SOME PERSISTENT QUESTIONS ON BEGINNING READING

ROBERT C. AUKERMAN, *Editor*
University of Rhode Island

INTERNATIONAL READING ASSOCIATION
Six Tyre Avenue Newark, Delaware 19711

Library of Congress Catalog Card Number: 73-190454
Second Printing, November 1973

CONTENTS

The International Reading Association attempts, through its publications, to provide a forum for a wide spectrum of opinion on reading. This policy permits divergent viewpoints without assuming the endorsement of the Association.

FOREWORD

Beginnings are important. During the formative years, especially in grades one to three, the child may or may not acquire reading skills commensurate with his maturational growth. But in either case, attitudes will be developed and once these are launched, they will gain a momentum and direction which will be difficult to control or redirect at a later time.

The well-known twenty-seven first grade studies did not indicate the superiority of one approach over others, but, when considered as one mammoth study with many facets, the studies did highlight again *the importance of the teacher.* The studies answered few, if any, of the perplexing problems faced by a teacher. They still plague her and she is constantly seeking ways and means by which she can organize a more viable reading/learning environment and strategies by which she can reorganize this learning atmosphere to provide for the different learning rates and problems manifested by the child.

This volume is an organized collection of papers which were presented at the International Reading Association convention at Atlantic City. The authors are scholars concerned with early childhood education. They explore topics that range from conclusions drawn from research on implicit speech to the advisability of teaching reading to preschoolers.

Some Persistent Questions on Beginning Reading is a volume that will be added to an impressive and timely list of IRA publications made available to teachers, administrators, supervisors, and laymen interested in the education of our youth.

A cursory glance at the table of contents will reveal at once the range and depth of the articles. The ultimate answers to these questions cannot be provided, but some of the best answers at this point in time are presented on such intriguing questions as the following: Is implicit speech (inner vocalization) a natural adjunct of the reading process? What are the components of a language arts program in the primary grades? What are some of the best measures for assessing readiness? What are some of the better strategies in preschool beginning reading programs? Are linguistic strategies better than traditional phonics in teaching reading?

A careful and reflective reading of the articles contained in this volume will be both provocative and informative. Until we find the final answers to these persistent questions, the reading of scholarly papers should be provocative and should stimulate the reader to explore, explore, explore. Your critical reading of these papers is invited. You will find it to be a rewarding experience.

Donald L. Cleland, *President*
International Reading Association
1970-1971

Robert C. Aukerman
University of Rhode Island

INTRODUCTION

The many variables comprising the process of learning to read from a printed page should convince any reasonable person that beginning reading is a multifaceted task. Yet, for decades there have been educational mystics who have sought answers through intuition and revelation and have gathered followers to their teachings. Wise Men from afar have appeared, bringing gifts of magic from their realms, and many in reading have bowed in awe. Alchemists and prescriptionists have conjured up new formulae that hold promises of shortcuts to beginning reading. Occasionally these persons have been commissioned to demonstrate their wizardries. And, now, many thoughtful and concerned members of the reading profession are calling for more definitive proofs of the existence of cause-and-effect relationships between strategies for achieving success in beginning reading and actual achievement.

More than one hundred approaches to beginning reading are presently available (*1*). Each claims success, yet few have research adequate to support their claims. Some approaches are built upon an oversimplified definition of reading. They view reading as merely "sounding out" words. Akin to this naïve concept is the idea that beginning reading skills can be taught through a highly structured sequential input of grapheme-phoneme correspondences isolated from meaningful context (*2*).

Some originators of beginning-to-read strategies subscribe to the opposite view: that reading is an integral part of the larger galaxy of language skills and, consequently, should not be separated from others. There is much to be said for the fact that if an individual can spell and write, he can read. Simplified spelling procedures and contrived orthographies have been used to produce faster results in beginning reading (*3*).

Composing sentences and paragraphs presupposes cognitive and, sometimes, affective input; and, conversely, the reading of sentences and paragraphs should assume that the printed material is making an impact upon the reader's cognitive and affective domains. To relegate beginning reading strategies merely to the domain of psychomotor skill development is to deprive both reader and author. Only in the most inept writing and/or in purposeful nonsense is it justifiable to teach phonics word attack skills under the assumption that transfer may later occur automatically. And, then, the teaching of pure phonics elements is seldom, if ever, accomplished in a vacuum, albeit some so-called research studies have reported "results" from "experiments" that have left all of the other variables uncontrolled.

Individualized reading, as an approach to beginning skill development, appeals to the child's own interests and motivation. As such, it subscribes to two basic principles of learning. Yet there are some practitioners, envisioning a classroom full of do-it-yourself six-year-old automatons, who have welcomed individualized reading as the long-awaited shortcut in beginning reading. Veatch (*5*) and Duker (*4*) delineate the elaborate strategies necessary for what a novice might superficially mistake as being a *laissez faire* operation.

The strategies purporting a cause-and-effect relationship to beginning reading and causing the greatest concern to practitioners in the profession are two: perceptual-discrimination kinaesiastics and structured preschool learning projects.

A growing number of professionals are maintaining that *perception* is their exclusive territory, chief among them are a large number of optometrists, some physiotherapists, specialists in the education of exceptional (physically handicapped) children, social scientists recently turned spokesmen for the disadvantaged, and those psychologists who have transferred their attentions from children with learning disabilities to children who are beginning to read.

Inasmuch as perception is the common denominator underlying their interests in beginning reading, it is not surprising to observe a common feature in the rituals they have devised for developing perception readiness for beginning reading. Perceptual training presupposes a direct relationship between it and the acquisition of beginning reading skills. The existence of such a causal relationship has been supported mainly by supposition.

It is not logical to continue perceptual-discrimination strategies on the assumption that they produce beginning-reading readiness or to dismiss them as being worthless in the absence of adequate proof that any significant correlation exists.

Strategies for teaching reading to preschool children elicit quite different responses and reactions—some logical, some emotional, and some promotional. In the latter instances, it appears that the objectives of some programs for training preschoolers to read are directed toward publicity, sensationalism, and/or the promotion of commercial materials. Emotional pleas for giving early instruction in reading to preschool children are frequently directed in favor of disadvantaged Black children while counter pleadings are emotionally charged with "preserve childhood" slogans. Logical reasons for teaching reading to four- and five-year-olds are more difficult to find; and when located, they seem to pervert logic by claiming that ". . . inasmuch as some children can learn to read at an early age, therefore. . . ." Unfortunately, some of the claimants for early reading instruction have excerpted partial findings from context or have misinterpreted the findings of selected research studies to support their own biases.

After more than a half century of reading research, it would seem that the reading profession would have definitive answers to its most persistent questions concerning beginning reading instruction. Some of the answers—or, at least, partial answers—may lie latent in the mountains of research data. But the questions still continue to arise, and many "answers" continue to confuse.

True, there are no closed, final, absolute answers to problems of human existence in an undulating pluralistic environment. But it is past time—and the reading profession is becoming insistent—that we have some tentative "best answers" to such questions as:

1. What constitutes the "best" readiness strategies?
2. What are some "best" measures of assessing readiness for beginning reading and/or for predicting reading failure?
3. Is it "best" to teach reading to preschoolers?
4. What strategies are "best" in preschool beginning-reading programs?
5. How may beginning-reading strategies be "best" integrated and articulated with the total language arts program?
6. Are there some "best" strategies for teaching phonics, decoding, blending, and other word-analysis skills to beginning readers?
7. Are linguistics strategies "better" than traditional phonics in teaching beginning reading?
8. What are the "best" answers to claims that auditory-perceptual-

discrimination training and visual-perceptual-discrimination training are significant factors in beginning reading?

9. Is silent reading the "best" strategy when language is essentially phonemic?

The papers contained here were selected because they provide some definitive "best answers" to those important questions.

References

1. Aukerman, Robert C. *Approaches to Beginning Reading.* New York: John Wiley and Sons, 1971.
2. Bloomfield, Leonard. "Linguistics and Reading," *Elementary English Review,* 19, 125-130, 183-186.
3. Downing, John A. "The i/t/a (Initial Teaching Alphabet) Reading Experiments," *Reading Teacher,* 18 (November 1964), 105-110.
4. Duker, Sam. *Individualized Reading.* Springfield, Illinois: Charles R. Thomas, 1971.
5. Veatch, Jeannette. *Reading in the Elementary School.* New York: Ronald Press, 1966.

WHAT CONSTITUTES THE "BEST" READINESS STRATEGIES?

Sam Leaton Sebesta
University of Washington

presents some strategies in storytelling, an essential element in the kindergarten readiness sequence.

THE ART OF STORYTELLING

Storytelling has survived the Gutenberg galaxy; it ought to survive the electronic age, too. It will survive accountability. Scheherezade, remember, was held accountable for telling a rouser every night for 1001 nights, under penalty of losing her head. Scheherezade did just fine, as did Odysseus who was, perhaps, a wilier storyteller than hero, though this trait did not detract from his magnetism.

There is evidence from McLuhan and others that we are heading toward a broader concept of comprehension—not just reading comprehension but the comprehension involved in *visual* literacy and in oracy. If this is the case, then the art of storytelling will gain in reputation. We need to examine the art carefully. Even in the midst of electronic wonders, storytelling is still one of the firmest avenues to comprehension that we possess.

Storytelling and Acting

Storytelling is often described in contrast to acting in the theater. The contrast may be superficial, arising from comparing good storytelling with bad acting. A good actor has learned to be three persons. First, he has learned to be the author of the play. He knows the structure of the play, and how it is going to turn out. He knows the theme or themes and how each scene fits into the whole. He recapitulates the author's process. This recapitulation overrides the segment of the play which is his own role, large or small.

Second, the actor has learned to be a character in the play. He *acts* out the character, we say, but it would be more accurate to say that he *interprets* the character. It is like the difference between a newsphoto and an Andrew Wyeth painting. The actor must interpret how the character fits into the whole pattern.

Third, the actor must learn to be part of the audience and watch the play unfold. In this function he does not know or unduly anticipate what will happen until it happens. He makes guesses and responds to false leads on the basis of what has gone before but not what is yet unknown.

Structuring the Story

Like the actor, the storyteller recapitulates the creative process of the author. As author, he knows how the story is going to turn out. He senses its structure, including elements such as conflict, climax, and denouement. Moreover, he is capable of living through the story again and again, as authors live their stories when they create them and as actors live through plays when they play them. Like the author, he must sense how and to what degree each segment fits into the whole pattern.

The storyteller is *all* the characters in the story, yet he is really none of them. His role playing is less direct, though by this indirection he aims for an effect similar to that of the actor. Like the actor, he entices his audience to catch the image of characters going about their businesses of living within the cause-and-effect of narrative. He, too, *interprets* characters.

And the storyteller is also the audience. The best storytellers have the grace and manner which says, "I know what you think will happen. I know your opinion of this and that character. I know the image in your mind. You want to know if you're right? Well, we'll just have to wait and see, won't we?"

This is the manner that persuaded Alice, of *Through the Looking Glass,* to believe six impossible things before breakfast. It invites camaraderie. Not all actors can manage it. Those who try and fail are called hams. There are, unfortunately, ham storytellers, too, who are spawned when audience-pleasing takes precedence over carrying out the author's intent and concentration on character. Mark Twain (*6*) describes the "ham" fallacy best in comparing the teller of a *humorous* story to the teller of a *comic* story:

> The humorous story is told gravely; the teller does his best to conceal the fact that he even dimly suspects that there is anything funny about it; but the teller of the comic story tells you before hand that it is one of the funniest things he has ever heard, then tells it with eager delight, and is the first person to laugh when he gets through. And sometimes, if he has

> had good success, he is so glad and happy that he will repeat the "nub" of it and glance around from face to face, collecting applause, and then repeat it again. It is a pathetic thing to see.

Twain concluded that witnessing such a performance "makes one want to renounce joking and lead a better life."

The Broadway production, *Story Theatre,* exemplifies the close relationship between actor and storyteller. The actors in this show effortlessly step out of character to tell the story, then just as effortlessly pick up the character again to dramatize. It can be done. The art, comprising intent, is very similar. The techniques of the storyteller and the actor, however, differ somewhat.

Technique of Storytelling

One technical suggestion for the storyteller says, "Don't memorize." This is a recent ruling. Storytellers in ancient times memorized, and some do so today. Greek schoolboys learned the *Odyssey.* Too many of us were forced to memorize the wrong way, and we got sick of it. But often when a story is worked on so that we recapitulate the author's process, the story begins to stick in the memory like a song. If memorized effortlessly in this way, the story is aided rather than blocked in the telling, as happens with favorite stories. The "rule" might be changed to say, "Don't memorize—if it hurts."

Another bit of technical advice might be phrased this way: "Don't use props and don't wave your arms about." Yet a prop can help. A leaf can make a forest. One authentic ax or ax model can bring focus on the blurred panorama of Ithaca. A prop can begin a story—"thereupon hangs a tale"—and it can supplant some tiresome description, but don't drag in a prop or use too many. See if one prop helps, though.

Arm waving, head wagging, and jumping up and down are certainly distractions to be avoided. But some storytellers are lifeless because all the action has been trained out of them. It seems somehow *disinteresting* to sit primly with one's hands carefully in place when one is conjuring a jolly tailor sewing up the sky with a hundred miles of thread to make the rain stop. It would be easy if we were all Ruth Sawyers or Gudrun Thorne-Thomsens or May Arbuthnots or Bill Martins—able to convey almost unbearable immediacy with our voices alone.

Shedlock (*3*) says that Anglo-Saxons move in solid blocks, that is, are gross in gestures. We cannot "gesture" getting on a horse without lifting a leg over our heads and clutching at something. But those of other cultures are artists of the gesture, and we can learn from them. An almost imperceptible movement of the head can say in Greece, "It is sunny and pleasant today. I am going to drink two glasses of retsina and enjoy the view. I hope you are enjoying it, too."

Shedlock says that we should learn sparing use of gesture, not non-use of gesture. This is important advice. If you are not Greek, you might begin grossly. Practice with big gestures that fit the story and gradually tame them down.

Of all techniques for aiding this art, voice technique is strongest. Two suggestions regarding vocal technique have proved useful: the use of *crescendo* and the use of the *pause*. Both can be planned ahead of time, even marked on the printed story or outline, and then practiced.

Crescendo is sometimes defined as "getting louder," but perhaps it is better described as "starting softer." There is a difference. If you start a story low-pitched and softly, you have some dynamics in reserve. If you must begin fortissimo in order to capture attention, find a place early in the story to retreat. Incidentally, this technique is known to good actors, too. We have all experienced the actor who seems great the first ten minutes but eventually makes us realize that there is no heightening of dramatic tension to come. In all art, as in life, much depends upon aroused expectations—what is to come, rather than the present.

Pause is also a means of arousing expectation. Twain in *How to Tell a Story* considers it indispensable. So do others. The pause lets the listener wonder and hope. It gives him a chance to be surprised.

Other voice techniques are so complex that they defy description, though some teachers of storytelling and acting know magically how to develop them.

A description of storytelling in Russia over the centuries says simply that "The telling of a tale is primarily an art, a special skill, accessible to the artists of the poetic word, to persons who are especially gifted for this kind of work" (*4*). Those gifted ones among Russian storytellers took their work seriously. They were in demand. The mills and market-places hired them to draw customers. These artists were not concerned about repeating a story. In fact, we are told that some had only two or three stories in their entire repertoire, but effective ones. They knew what to do with gesture, pause, and voice. In 1649 they were adjudged *so* effective that a royal rescript to governors commanded severest penalties for storytelling. As reported by Sokolov (*4*), the edict read in part:

> Many men senselessly believe in dreams, in encounters, and in the evil eye, and in the calling of birds, and they propound riddles and tell tales of things unheard-of, and by idle talk and merry-making, in blasphemy they destroy their souls with such benighted deeds. For all this the most serene Tsar commands the governors to impose the severest penalties.

Few of us can pose so great a threat today. Those who can, have, by gift and practice, learned to beguile with words just as a ballet dancer has learned to climb the air to beguile with movement. The storyteller shortens the distance between words and feelings, between a word and its referent. Ultimately, this art eludes technique.

If it is really such an elusive art, should a teacher or librarian or parent attempt it? Shouldn't we rely on recordings or, with luck, locate the town storyteller? Those might be good things to do, but they are not substitutes. Children respond best to a voice they know, to a voice performing for them "at a given time in a given place" (*1*). If our voices bring only half the magic, children will bring the other half.

Shedlock suggests that we learn seven stories a year—just seven—and see how over the years these become a fine repertoire. Mae Benne at the University of Washington makes another useful suggestion: Have each teacher learn to tell *one* story and at an appointed hour each week have teachers rotate to tell their stories to different classrooms. The class is maintained, and the offering is vastly multiplied. This is a good way to get started.

Should children tell stories? There is never any doubt that they *do*—personal experiences, movie and television shows, and more. It may be surprising to learn that at the turn of the century there arose a whole movement to encourage children to repeat a story after it was told by the teacher. Various claims were made for this practice: that it contributed to good speech and good listening, that it increased knowledge of literature, and the like.

Nowadays we are less enthusiastic over such close modeling, although a teacher shouldn't be surprised to learn that children go home and repeat a story at the dinner table. In 1913, McManus said, "Storytelling is superior to the written story chiefly because the man who writes is not in touch with the audience. The storyteller talks to you and has to make a story from beginning to end, and every sentence has to be a part of the story, because he is within range of a brickbat—and subject to the recall at any minute" (*2*).

Children respond well to practice and guidance in storytelling. With a little thought and manipulation of words, a teacher should have no difficulty in providing accountability in this matter. Make sure to provide access to good stories to tell.

Elementary English from time to time is a useful source (*5*). If one pupil tells a story to an entire class, practice is limited and attention is sometimes strained. It is better to divide a class into groups of three or four and have storytellers all around the room and in the corridor. Incidentally, encouragement to tell stories in childhood will most certainly pay off in adulthood. We hope to increase our status as a nation of readers. We can become a nation of storytellers, too.

Storytelling is tough fibered. Stories hold the reins of continuity and the consciousness of all cultures, even the whole unified theme of civilization. Stories live on, even when history is forgotten. There can be no doubt that storytelling is strong enough to survive history itself.

References

1. Chambers, Dewey W. "Storytelling: The Neglected Art," *Elementary English*, 43 (November 1966), 715-719+.

2. Forbush, William Byron. *Storytelling in the Home*. American Institute of Child Life, 1913, 5.

3. Shedlock, Marie L. *The Art of the Story-Teller*. New York: Dover Publications, 1915, 1951.

4. Sokolov, Y. M. *Russian Folklore*, translated by Catherine Ruth Smith. New York: Macmillan, 1950, 400.

5. Thornley, Gwendella. "Storytelling is Fairy Gold," *Elementary English*, 40 (January 1968), 67-79+.

6. Twain, Mark. "How to Tell a Story," *Mark Twain's Works*, Volume 22 (Underwood edition). Hartford, Connecticut: American Publishing Company, 1901.

JAMES T. FLEMING
State University of New York at Albany

discusses strategies for developing the language skills of preschool children.

PROMOTING LANGUAGE SKILLS IN PRESCHOOL PROGRAMS

Of all the substantive concerns related to preschool programs, language skills continue to be prominently considered. This central concern for promoting language skills is understandable; for, through its many uses, language functions as the medium for a large part of instruction and learning in both formal and informal settings during the earliest years of any child's life.

Recent concern for preschool language development is, possibly, the result of 1) studies of childrens' language acquisitions which have incorporated major changes in investigative approach as well as in linguistic theory, both of which have become more widely known only within the past decade; 2) notions of what constitutes readiness for intellectual activities which have increasingly received sophisticated, interdisciplinary attention; and 3) the demands of many heretofore rather quiet segments of society which have challenged many underlying assumptions, overt practices, and apparent outcomes of traditional preschool activities.

In addition, much of the major thrust has been concerned with the preschool language development of the population which usually is labeled "disadvantaged." This concentration seems to be reasonable, inasmuch as a preoccupation with language skills frequently prompts the most controversy in preschool programs for disadvantaged children.

Different vs Deficient Language

Particularly within the past five years or so, the overriding controversy relating to disadvantaged children's language can most economically be traced to and described as the *deficiency vs difference* issue. Essentially, adherents of a "deficiency" point of view would use such phrases as "nonverbal," "verbally deprived," and even the term "verbally destitute" to describe Black ghetto children's language. Cazden (5) recently referred to this issue in the following cogent manner:

> The school language problems of lower-class children can have two explanations: either they have acquired less language than middle-class children, or they have acquired a different language. The less-language explanation has been given various names—*cultural deprivation, deficit hypothesis, vacuum ideology*—all with the same connotation of a nonverbal child somehow emptier of language than his more socially fortunate age-mates.

This deficit hypothesis or "deficiency" point of view has been most obvious in the writings and programs of such individuals as Deutsch (*7*) and Bereiter and Engelmann (*2*). In this same context, it might be noted that Bernstein's early and widely disseminated speculations on "elaborated" and "restricted" codes also, at least indirectly, tended to support a deficit hypothesis (*3*). Taken in its extreme form, many individuals were inclined to interpret Bereiter's views as indicative of the possibility that some Black children possess "no language at all" or, at least, no language worth serious consideration.

Prominent among those who have increasingly opposed the deficit hypothesis are Baratz and Shuy (*1*), Labov (*12*), and Stewart (*15*), all of whom have insisted, for example, that the Black ghetto child's language is neither more nor less deficient than any other form of speech but that it is, in fact, simply different. All of these individuals have conducted intensive studies of some Black dialects, and their findings are indisputable: these nonstandard forms reflect a formally structured linguistic system, and consequently, should not be viewed as abnormal deviations from the norms of standard English. In effect, this form of nonstandard speech is not merely a bundle of random "errors"; nor is it some primitive, half-formed, or incomplete system incapable of allowing its user to express any experienced idea or feeling.

Linguistic vs Communicative Competence

How then might one move toward a reconciliation of *deficiency vs different* points of view; for clearly neither position alone represents an acceptable position because, in this writer's opinion, neither position alone accords well with theory or reality. In this regard, it is truly unfortunate that until rather recently, this divisiveness has been exacerbated further by several tenets of Chomsky, one of this country's most distinguished theorists in linguistics. Although the related technical aspects of his writings need not detain us here, it is important to note that 1) In a widely quoted passage, Chomsky (*6*) claims that

> Linguistic theory is concerned primarily with an ideal speaker-listener, in a completely homogeneous speech-community, who knows its language perfectly and is unaffected by such grammatically irrelevant conditions as memory limitations, distractions, shifts of attention and interest, and errors (random or characteristic) in applying his knowledge of the language in actual performance.

and 2) few linguists accept the deficiency point of view, regardless of whether they agree wholly, in part, or not at all with Chomsky's notions. A few years ago Hymes, another well-known linguist, faced this issue and insightfully and elegantly suggested a resolution. As a participant at Yeshiva University in a research planning conference on language development in disadvantaged children, Hymes (*10*) referred to Chomsky's ideal speaker-listener model with the following remarks:

> When the image of the unfolding, mastering, fluent child is set beside the real children in many of our schools, the theoretical basis of the image is seen for what it is, not a *doctrine of irrelevance,* but a *doctrine of poignancy.* Such theory is based on the essential equality and potential of each child in his or her capacity simply as a human being. It is noble in that it can inspire one with the belief that even the most dispiriting conditions can be transformed; and it is an indispensable weapon against views which would explain the communicative difficulties of groups of children as inherent, perhaps racial.

Hymes also suggested that the scope of an important distinction in linguistic theory be broadened. Much has been written about the distinction between linguistic *competence* and linguistic *performance,* wherein the former conventionally has been restricted to the speaker's tacit or intuitive knowledge of language and the latter to the use he makes of that knowledge in concrete situations. The dilemma for most individuals seriously concerned with language and language use evolved as a result of a theoretical or logical point which seemed to be insisted upon—namely, that performance could not be satisfactorily explained or understood without a prior and equally satisfactory explication of the assumed underlying competence. In recognizing the equally poignant inadequacy of such a narrow view, Hymes (*10*) suggests that any useful theory of communicative competence should be built around the observation that:

> Data from very early in life, the first years of acquisition of grammar, show children do develop rules for the use of different forms in different situations . . . . Competency for use is part of the same developmental matrix as competency for grammar. . . . Within the developmental matrix in which children acquire the knowledge in principle of the set of sentences of a language they also acquire the knowledge in principle of a set of ways in which sentences are used; and they internalize attitudes toward a language and it [sic] uses, and indeed, toward language itself (including, e.g., attentiveness to it) or its place in a pattern of mental abilities.

From a theoretical point of view, Hymes' suggestion [which now is more fully developed in a more recent publication (*11*)] is most important; from a practical point of view, his suggestion acknowledges what many good teachers have long known: the social context of learning, particularly language learning, is at least as important as the specific aim of the activity; and some consideration and understanding of this oft-neglected situation may go a long way toward enabling children to proceed profitably in oral language situations at the preschool level and well into the elementary grades (*5*).

Language Form and Language Use

To cite one distinction with wideranging implications especially for practices in preschool settings, some understanding of the considerations mentioned may lead us to pay less heed to language form and more to language use. It may allow us to better structure school situations wherein children's language will come into use, provided we are constantly and consistently mindful of some simple yet necessary prerequisites for children's language to be used. Some very obvious factors which have been noted often include ". . . adult participation, something concrete to talk about, physical arrangements, and noise" (*4*). Similar considerations may force us to move away from a position where we might insist that a child *can't* (is incapable of or has no capacity to) use his language for any number of situations to a position where we assume the burden of discovering why he *doesn't* (or isn't in the habit of using his language in this or that manner) and then set about trying to remedy the situation. In short, our assumptions regarding children's language *use* should be more open and optimistic, and our concerns for the *form* of the language should, with some exceptions, come to occupy a singularly second-rated priority.

"Proper" Form vs Productive Use

In this context, there are many clues to be found in *Language Face to Face* (*9*). One of the reports in this collection of papers provides an account by San Jose (*14*) of her observations while visiting some primary schools in Leicestershire. The response to her questions concerning "standard dialect"—the extent to which it was preferred and the manner and frequency with which it was taught—illustrates a refreshing point of view:

> In the evening I brought up the subject with a teacher of six- to seven-year olds in what might be called a very underprivileged neighborhood. She obviously considered the dialect question of minimal importance. "Well, you're thankful to get them writing and talking at all, aren't you?" was her reaction. As I pursued the matter, she said that sometimes she would point out the most glaring discrepancies, in written work, to the brightest children. But she would rather accept "I ain't done now" and go on from there than hold up proceedings—perhaps stop them dead—insisting on "I haven't done anything." She was adamant about work habits, especially perseverance, and classroom manners; she considered teaching a social responsibility, not just a pedagogical task. But apparently dialect wasn't worrying her.

Conclusions

Is it just possible that the British, with particular regard to the philosophy, aims, and practices of early childhood programs, have been more able than we in this country to move away from a preoccupation with "proper language forms" to a more defensible concern for extended, productive language use? No matter what the verdict here, two brief comments from others may sum up much of the central focus of this paper.

Early (*9*) notes:

> Accountability is as much on our minds these days as openness and freedom. We do not believe that the concepts are incompatible. But having seen the effects on teachers and children of a narrow accounting of skills acquisition in just one phase of language development, we would urge a concept of accountability that measures not only learning but zest for learning.

Her words serve as a timely echo of one of Loban's concise contributions (*13*): ". . . if your evaluation is narrow and mechanical, this is what the curriculum will be."

These two comments could well be constant reminders that no curriculum for early childhood schooling should reflect the narrow or the mechanical, for this state of affairs represents the antithesis of any hope for promoting useful language skills.

References

1. Baratz, Joan, and Roger Shuy. (Eds.). *Teaching Black Children to Read*. Washington, D.C.: Center for Applied Linguistics, 1969.
2. Bereiter, Carl, and Siegfried Engelmann. *Teaching Disadvantaged Children in the Preschool*. Englewood Cliffs, New Jersey: Prentice-Hall, 1966.
3. Bernstein, Basil. "Elaborated and Restricted Codes: Their Social Origins and Some Consequences," in A. G. Smith (Ed.), *Communication and Culture*. New York: Holt, Rinehart and Winston, 1966.
4. Cazden, Courtney. "Environmental Assistance to the Child's Acquisition of Grammar," unpublished doctoral dissertation, Harvard University, 1965.
5. Cazden, Courtney. "The Neglected Situation in Child Language Research and Education," in Frederick Williams (Ed.), *Language and Poverty,* Institute for Research on Poverty Monograph Series. Chicago: Markham Publishing Company, 1970, 81-101.
6. Chomsky, Noam. *Aspects of the Theory of Syntax*. Cambridge, Massachusetts: MIT Press, 1965.
7. Deutch, Martin, and associates. *The Disadvantaged Child*. New York: Basic Books, 1967.
8. Dixon, John. *Growth Through English* (A report based on the Dartmouth Seminar 1966). Reading, England: National Association for the Teaching of English, 1967.
9. Early, Margaret (Ed.). *Language Face to Face*. Syracuse, New York: Reading and Language Arts Center, Syracuse University, 1971.
10. Hymes, Dell. "On Communicative Competence," *Research Planning Conference on Language Development in Disadvantaged Children*. New York: Ferkauf Graduate School of Humanities and Social Sciences, Yeshiva University, 1964.
11. Hymes, Dell. "On Communicative Competence," in R. Huxley and E. Ingram (Eds.), *The Mechanisms of Language Development*. London, England: CIBA Foundation, 1971.

12. Labov, William. "The Logic of Nonstandard English," in James Alatis (Ed.), *Twentieth Annual Round Table Meeting on Languages and Linguistics Studies,* Monograph Series No. 22, 1969. Washington, D.C.: Georgetown University Press, 1970, 1-43.

13. Loban, Walter, as quoted by John Dixon, in *Growth Through English* (a report based on the Dartmouth Seminar 1966). Reading, England: National Association for the Teaching of English, 1967, 92.

14. San Jose, Christine. "Language Throughout the Integrated Day," in Margaret Early (Ed.), *Language Face to Face.* Syracuse, New York: Reading and Language Arts Center, Syracuse University, 1971, 89-106.

15. Stewart, William. "Urban Negro Speech: Sociolinguistic Factors Affecting English Teaching," in R. W. Shuy (Ed.), *Social Dialects and Language Learning.* Champaign, Illinois: National Council of Teachers of English, 1965, 10-18.

Jo M. Stanchfield
Occidental College

provides some specific answers in the form of developmental readiness strategies.

DEVELOPMENT OF PREREADING SKILLS IN AN EXPERIMENTAL KINDERGARTEN PROGRAM

Basic to the current approaches in teaching reading are the assumptions that success in beginning reading is crucial and that reading programs in the primary grades must be organized to assure that success. Evidence of the importance of achievement in initial reading instruction may be found in the large number of research studies designed to find more effective ways of teaching beginning reading and in the relatively recent concentration of research projects in reading readiness. *Sesame Street,* through the powerful teaching medium of television, has greatly increased the interest of the nation in prereading skills. This innovative program accepts the premise that the prekindergarten years are a period holding a potential for substantial and significant intellectual development (*5*). The show has adopted the techniques and approaches of commercial television to help preschoolers develop skills necessary to a successful start in formal reading instruction.

Recent Projects in Reading Readiness

An increasing number of authorities in early childhood education have recognized that children's formal education can and, perhaps, should begin long before the traditional age of five or six. Many recent studies in readiness have been conducted with children of ages three or four in structured learning situations.

In research reported by Karnes in 1968, a traditional nursery school program was compared with a highly structured program focused on specific learning tasks designed to promote language and cognitive development. Four-year-olds were studied in order that follow-up evaluation could be coordinated in public school kindergartens. At the end of the experimental period, results of the Metropolitan Readiness Test showed superior performance by the experimental group in both reading readiness and numbers readiness. The University of Illinois researchers concluded that their findings illustrated the effectiveness of teaching specific content as well as school readiness (*4*).

A four-year study conducted in New York by di Lorenzo and Salter studied the effectiveness of an academic year preschool program for the disadvantaged on a longitudinal basis, prekindergarten through second grade. The project encompassed eight school districts with a basic curriculum approach that emphasized language and cognitive development and varied in comprehensiveness and methods of reading readiness instruction. At the end of the first two years of the study, it was found that the prekindergarten experience had proven beneficial for the subjects and that the most effective prekindergarten programs were those with the most specific, structured cognitive activities (*3*).

Much recent research in reading readiness has been done with the culturally and economically deprived because they lack the background with which middle- or upper-class children begin their formal educations. Traditional preschool classes are not adequate to prepare the disadvantaged child to compete with children of more privileged environments. Thus, the gains reported for disadvantaged children in structured reading readiness programs contrast significantly with results in a California study by Prendergast comparing the development of prereading skills in three groups of upper-middle-class children, a conventional day nursery class, a Montessori preschool class, and a nonnursery school group. The conventional school offered common enrichment experiences while the Montessori class provided a structured program to develop skills through the use of special methods and materials. At the end of seven months, children were compared on development of perceptual-motor skills and receptive language. In most areas evaluated no significant differences were found among the three groups. The researcher attributed this result primarily to the fact that the upper-middle-class home environments encouraged the development of reading readiness skills without nursery school experience (*6*).

Investigators at the University of Iowa studied the effectiveness of the Frostig perceptual-motor method in developing reading readiness among 108 disadvantaged kindergarten children. The results of approximately eight months of training in sensorimotor and visual-perceptual exercises are reported by Alley in *Exceptional Children,* September 1968. Results, as measured by the Marianne Frostig Development Test of Visual Perception and the Metropolitan Readiness Test Form A, disclose significant differences in favor of the experimental group (*1*).

The "nature vs. nurture" controversy was considered by Bernabei in developing a reading readiness program in the Bucks County, Pennsylvania, schools. Do children grow into readiness, or is this goal rather a function of training and experience? Bernabei saw no immediate resolution of the controversy and undertook an interim, eclectic approach—an extended reading readiness program organized to cover a longer period of time than the standard kindergarten treatment. The program devised pupil learning experiences and developed materials related to a curriculum of readiness skills, including prereading and mathematics. An evaluation of the program after one year indicates significant differences in these skills between the interim class and the normal class (*2*).

Background and Objectives of the Research

Each year over the past seven years, the writer has been engaged in research in the Los Angeles City Schools with approximately 500 first grade children of varying ethnic and socioeconomic backgrounds. The purpose of the research has been to experiment with a variety of material and methods in teaching beginning reading to determine the effect upon the reading achievement of first grade children. During these years, it has become increasingly apparent to the writer, the teachers, and the administrators in the series of studies that there are certain prereading skills necessary for children to succeed in reading. Many children are not able to acquire proficiency in the reading readiness skills in the time ordinarily allotted in the first grade.

With this knowledge and with that from other reading readiness studies, the writer worked with teachers and administrators to develop a research design to teach these skills in sequential, developmental order: 1) listening for comprehension of content, 2) listening for auditory discrimination, 3) visual-discrimination skills, 4) oral-language skills, 5) motor-perceptual skills, and 6) sound-symbol-correspondence skills.

Through grouping and independent activities, specific lessons in the six areas were taught to small groups of children. The skills of each lesson were developed in detail in the teacher's manual. These skills were taught and retaught during practice periods until an adequate level of proficiency was attained by the children. The objective of the study was to determine whether children taught prereading skills in a structured program would attain significantly higher scores on a standardized test of reading readiness skills than those children who had not been involved in such a program.

Procedures

For the experimental program, seventeen schools were selected to provide a cross-section of socioeconomic levels representing ethnic categories of Black, Mexican-American, and other White children. Each experimental school was matched with a control school containing children of similar ethnic origins, academic achievement, and socioeconomic backgrounds. The teachers in both the experimental and control schools were randomly selected.

The teachers in the experimental program were given a teacher's guide for the reading readiness lessons and materials to implement their teaching. The specific prereading skills were taught in the language arts block of time in the kindergarten program. During the fall semester, those teachers met each week after school at a designated school building to receive additional materials and to discuss the use of materials. At these workshop-type meetings, the teachers also made instructional aids such as puppets and flannelboard activities from patterns provided.

The teachers in the control schools followed the regular kindergarten curricula which they had been previously teaching.

Materials and Techniques

The teaching philosophy of the program was established upon the premise that the skills in the reading process are the same on the prereading level as at the highest stage of reading development, the chief differences being those of degree and refinement. Therefore, the materials and techniques used in the research were developed to be parallel to the formal reading instruction that the children would receive as they progressed through the primary grades.

The materials for the program included:

I. The Teacher's Manual

Lesson plans were classified according to the six major areas of prereading skills, with improvement of one of those skills being the major purpose of each lesson.

Each lesson plan included six sections: a) purpose, b) preparation, c) presentation, d) evaluation of purpose, e) pupil practice materials, and f) additional experiences.

Preparation included materials needed in the presentation of the lesson. *Evaluation* consisted of a quick check of whether the children achieved the purpose of the lesson. *Pupil Practice Materials* provided independent follow-up exercises for reinforcement of the skills taught in the lesson. At the close of the lesson, *Additional Experiences* suggested activities related to the same skill as the one for which the specific plan was given.

II. Picture cards

Picture cards were used in a variety of ways: to stimulate imagination, to help in noting details, for picture reading, for storytelling, as inspiration for painting, motivation for dramatic play, and as stimulation for creative language, including stories dictated to the teacher.

III. Large flannelboard and pocket chart

The large flannelboard and pocket chart were big enough to be seen by a group of children. They were used by either the teacher or a child. The flannelboard held cutouts of story characters, objects, letters, and numbers. The pocket chart served as another illustrative aid.

IV. Individual flannelboard, pocket chart, and chalkboard

Small flannelboards, pocket charts, and chalkboards were available for each child in a group. Small groups were formed on the basis of specific needs. The teacher used individual manipulative materials to involve every child in the activity and learning and to obtain instant feedback on individual progress.

V. Flannelboard cutouts

Cutouts of the characters and objects from a story were used on the large flannelboard to illustrate a story when telling or retelling it. Other cutouts were used in teaching about a) shape, size, and color; b) sight-sound-symbol correspondence; and c) numerals and simple number concepts.

VI. Hand puppets

By using hand puppets children often overcome their self-consciousness. They are intent upon manipulating the puppet appropriately and "become" the puppet character. In the experimental program, puppets were used to motivate oral language, both for retelling a story and for creating new stories and conversations.

VII. Books

Books for the program were chosen primarily because of their universal appeal to four-, five-, and six-year-olds. Other criteria the books met were those of high literary quality, worthwhile illustrations, and appropriate format. The collection was comprised of a variety of categories, including Mother Goose, poetry, fairy or folktales, animal stories, an ABC book, and song books.

VIII. Phoneme boxes with small objects

Each box contained small objects, most of whose names began with one of the consonants. In the same box were a few objects whose names began with a different consonant. Children said the names of the objects and decided which ones started like a certain word from a preprimer and which to retain in the box.

The Development of Skills

An overview of the reading readiness program is shown in the following outline listing the six major skills and the teaching techniques employed in developing them.

I. Listening for comprehension of content

The ability to listen often is taken for granted and, therefore, is seldom specifically taught. Efficient listening must be practiced and learned. Because listening is so important to speech, language, and reading, special attention was given to this area in the research program.

The purposes of the lessons in this part of the experimental curriculum were listening for pleasure and relaxation, comprehending what someone read or said, memorizing, remembering, and following directions. The children listened to poems, songs, and recordings with an awareness of mood; as the teacher read or told a story they listened to answer directed questions or to recall and retell parts of the story; they listened to and followed simple, and later, more complex directions.

II. Listening for auditory discrimination and development

As a prelude to the aural discrimination of words and word elements, the children had many directed-listening experiences. After they learned to listen to the teacher, to one another, to music, and to sounds in their environment, the teacher began the development of the concepts of volume, pitch, direction, duration, sequence, accent, tempo, repetition, contrast, and distance. The teacher used a variety of recordings, tonal instruments, poems, jingles, and rhythms to develop those concepts.

III. Visual discrimination and development

Observing and interpreting content. The interpretation of pictures and picture stories helped children to develop such skills as arranging items in sequence, making inferences, predicting outcomes, getting the main idea, and noting relevant details.

Prior to this part of the program, the teachers organized school excursions and walking trips to give children opportunities to observe and become acquainted with the world beyond their immediate neighborhood. Those firsthand experiences helped the children to understand concepts represented in the pictures and picture stories which otherwise might have had no meaning.

Visual imagery. Visual projection, or recognition of an object from its description, was developed through such techniques as having the children guess the answers to riddles about familiar objects, paint pictures from vivid descriptions, or illustrate stories. Visual memory was practiced by the children through a variety of simple exercises such as describing objects or scenes from memory or by locating, with eyes shut, familiar objects in the room.

Visual discrimination. The children were taught to note gross likenesses and differences before making finer discriminations. Picture-matching games and the comparing and contrasting of pictures, objects, and geometric forms were used to help the children make discriminations of size, shape, position, color, and small details. The development of those concepts laid a foundation for the further study of visual skills.

IV. Oral language skills

The teachers provided experience in several areas related to oral expression: the ability to express ideas understandably to others; the ability to speak with the expression that conveys ideas and with pleasing voice quality; the use of complete and well-structured sentences; the expansion of speaking and understanding vocabularies; and the improvement of pronunciation and diction.

Varied and stimulating opportunities were provided for practice in oral expression. These ranged from spontaneous discussion of personal experiences to participation in creative storytelling, recitation of poems, or choral speaking.

V. Motor-perceptual development

Through directed lessons, the children learned to coordinate vision and movement, to become aware of and to manipulate the parts of their bodies, and to perceive positions of objects in relation to themselves. They learned body control through exercises, games, dances, and the interpretation of music. Later, opportunities for the development of finer motor coordination were provided through activities in construction, cutting, pasting, tracing, and coloring. Eventually the children were ready for paper and pencil exercises to further refine eye-hand coordination.

VI. Sound-symbol correspondence

In the experimental classes, sound-symbol correspondence was developed on levels of increasing difficulty. Practice was given to reinforce the learning of the sounds associated with the alphabet letters. Aural and visual recognitions, as well as letter discrimination, were stressed by association of pure letter sounds with the corresponding names and symbols, using objects and pictures. In the last step in the development of this skill, the children learned to write the various letters of the alphabet in manuscript form.

Counting from one to ten was presented in the same sequence as letter recognition.

Results of the Research

The Murphy-Durrell Reading Readiness Analysis was given to the seventeen experimental classes and the seventeen control classes at the end of the school year. A three-way analysis of variance was performed with sex, experimental control, and ethnic group as the main effects. The scores from the five tests of the Murphy-Durrell Analysis were studied separately and in total. When the F test was significant, it was followed by T tests between the groups.

TABLE 1

MEAN SCORES FOR EXPERIMENTAL AND CONTROL GROUPS ON MURPHY-DURRELL READING READINESS ANALYSIS

Group	Phonemes Test Part 1	Phonemes Test Part 2	Letter-Names Test Part 1	Letter-Names Test Part 2	Learning Rate Test	Total
Experimental	15.92	18.57	20.51	21.71	10.80	87.50
Control	11.98	12.62	14.24	16.66	7.54	63.05

Table 1 shows that the experimental group achieved a higher score than was achieved by the control group in the total test and also in all of the individual parts of the test.

TABLE 2
MEAN SCORES BY SEX ON MURPHY-DURRELL READING READINESS ANALYSIS

Group	Phonemes Test Part 1	Phonemes Test Part 2	Letter-Names Test Part 1	Letter-Names Test Part 2	Learning Rate Test	Total
Boys	13.72*	14.84	17.00*	18.35	8.64	72.56
Girls	14.19*	16.35	17.75*	20.01	9.70	77.99

* Differences on Phonemes Test Part 1 and Letter-Names Test Part 1 not statistically significant; i.e., could be due to chance.

Table 2 indicates that the girls as a group achieved higher scores than the boys in the total test as well as in the individual parts of the test. However, this difference might be due to chance in the first parts of the phoneme and letter-names sections of the test.

TABLE 3
MEAN SCORES FOR ETHNIC GROUPS ON MURPHY-DURRELL READING READINESS ANALYSIS

Group	Phonemes Test Part 1	Phonemes Test Part 2	Letter-Names Test Part 1	Letter-Names Test Part 2	Learning Rate Test	Total
Black	13.19	14.43	16.78	18.62	8.20	71.21
Mexican-Amer.	13.45	14.91	16.57	18.45	8.87	72.24
Other White	15.21	17.45	18.78	20.49	10.43	82.38

Table 3 indicates that the children in the other White group scored higher on the total test and in all individual parts of the test than did the Mexican-American and the Black children. While the Mexican-Americans achieved a higher overall average than the Black children, the latter group was slightly higher in both parts of the letter-names test.

Table 4 shows the means for the total test, separated according to the three main effects: experimental-control, sex, and ethnic group. Table 5 gives the analysis of covariance for those three main effects and their possible combinations. A check was made to see if the means shown in Tables 1, 2, 3, and 4 were significantly different.

TABLE 4
MEANS FOR TOTAL SCORE ON MURPHY-DURRELL READING READINESS ANALYSIS

	Black	Mexican-American	Other White
Boys	67.68	69.37	80.64
Girls	74.73	75.11	84.12
Total	71.21	72.24	82.38
	Black	**Mexican-American**	**Other White**
Experimental	82.68	84.57	95.27
Control	59.73	59.92	69.49
Total	71.21	72.24	82.38
	Boys	**Girls**	**Total**
Experimental	86.04	88.97	87.50
Control	59.09	67.00	63.05
Total	72.56	77.99	75.28

TABLE 5
ANALYSIS OF COVARIANCE FOR TOTAL SCORES ON MURPHY-DURRELL READING READINESS ANALYSIS

Source of Variation	Sum of Squares	D.F.	Mean Square	F	P
Experimental-Control	205120.56	1	205120.56	315.28	0.00
Sex	10089.19	1	10089.19	15.51	0.00
Ethnic	34876.29	2	17438.14	26.80	0.00
Exp.-Con. × Sex	2122.16	1	2122.16	3.26	0.07
Exp.-Con. × Ethnic	464.45	2	232.22	.36	0.70
Sex × Ethnic	764.55	2	382.27	0.59	0.56
Exp.-Con. × Sex × Ethnic	714.53	2	357.27	0.55	0.58

Note: Column P gives the probability of differences occurring by chance. Normally, if P is equal to or less than .05, one can say that it would not happen by chance; i.e., it is significant.

It was found that all three main effects showed significant differences:

1. The experimental groups achieved significantly higher scores than the control groups.
2. The girls, as a group, achieved significantly better than the boys in the study.

3. The other White group achieved significantly higher scores than the Mexican-American and the Black groups. It should be pointed out that the experimental Mexican-American and Black groups achieved considerably higher scores than the control group of other White.

Table 5 also shows that combinations of the various possible groupings did not produce additional significant differences; that is, although the three main effects were significant, the interactions between the groups were not significant.

Conclusion

In summary, it may be said that the children in the kindergartens who were being taught in a structured, sequential program with appropriate materials achieved significantly more reading readiness skills than the children in the regular kindergarten curricula.

References

1. Alley, G., and others. "Reading Readiness and the Frostig Training Program," *Exceptional Children,* 35 (September 1968), 68.

2. Bernabei, R. "An Evaluation of the Interim Class: An Extended Readiness Program," unpublished research, Bucks County, Pennsylvania, Public Schools, 1967.

3. di Lorenzo, L. J., and R. Salter. "An Evaluative Study of Prekindergarten Programs for Educationally Disadvantaged Children: Follow Up and Replication," *Exceptional Children,* 35 (October 1968), 111-119.

4. Karnes, Merle B., and others. "Evaluation of Two Preschool Programs for Disadvantaged Children: A Traditional and a Highly Structured Experimental Preschool," *Exceptional Children,* 34 (May 1968), 667-676.

5. Palmer, E. L. "Can Television Really Teach? Preschoolers Watch *Sesame Street* Series," *American Education,* 5 (August 1969), 2-6.

6. Prendergast, R. "Prereading Skills Developed in Montessori and Conventional Nursery Schools," *Elementary School Journal,* 70 (December 1969), 135-141.

WHAT ARE SOME "BEST" MEASURES OF ASSESSING READINESS FOR BEGINNING READING AND/OR FOR PREDICTING READING FAILURE?

Warren Askov, Wayne Otto, and Richard Smith
University of Wisconsin

report on a study of the increment of predictability contributed by certain tests.

ASSESSMENT OF THE DE HIRSCH PREDICTIVE INDEX TESTS OF READING FAILURE

The purpose of the present three-year study was to investigate the predictive validity and the general usability in a school setting of a battery of ten tests reported to be predictors of reading failure by de Hirsch, Jansky, and Langford (*1*).

The need for further study of the de Hirsch Predictive Index Tests of Reading Failure seemed apparent for a number of reasons. First, the subjects in the de Hirsch study were a select group that did not represent the wide range of mental ability in most kindergarten classes.

Second, in the de Hirsch study the predictive battery was administered in a clinical setting which might produce results different from those which would be obtained in a more typical school setting.

Third, of the 53 subjects in the de Hirsch study only 6 were judged to be "less-than-adequate" readers and only 5 were judged to be "poor" readers at the end of second grade. Furthermore, 5 of those judged to be less-than-adequate readers at the end of second grade scored as the 2.5 to 3.4 grade level on the Gates Advanced Primary Test and 2.4 or below on the Gray Oral Reading Test, scores which mean that they may have been considered adequate readers by other judges' standards.

Finally, although de Hirsch, Jansky, and Langford report their study to be "preliminary in nature," their battery of ten tests has been cited in the professional literature dealing with the prevention and correction of reading disability (*2, 3*) and is reportedly already being used with some modification in public schools. Impatience to report, to cite, and to use the results of a preliminary study attests to the interest in the effort to predict reading failure and emphasizes the need for immediate and thorough investigation of the de Hirsch battery.

Methods

Selection of Subjects

The de Hirsch battery was administered to 433 kindergarten children, average age five years, ten months, at six Madison Public Schools. In order to determine the feasibility of using the de Hirsch tests with children of varied characteristics, no attempt was made to prescreen the children for ability, SES, or other variables.

Experimental Variables

Kindergarten tests. Data collected in kindergarten consisted of age, sex, scores on the ten tasks of the de Hirsch predictive index, and scores on a word association task which had previously been found to be related to reading ability in older children. Two of the ten tests de Hirsch et al. originally administered individually were group administered in the present study. They were Bender Visual-Motor Gestalt test and the Word Matching subtest of the Gates Reading Readiness battery. Those two tests were given to intact kindergarten classes by the same examiner and one of two assistants. With the exception of the group administration of those two tests, the content and administration of all tests were essentially similar to the description by de Hirsch et al. The remaining tests, administered individually, involved 1) ability to hold a pencil, 2) Wepman Auditory Discrimination Task, 3) number of words used to tell *The Three Bears* story, 4) providing generic category names for three groups of words, 5) a word reversals task, and 6) recognition and reproduction of two words previously taught. A word association task was added in which a child was asked to give his first association to each of seven words. The associations were scored in terms of consensuality with all associations given. High consensuality received a high score. Each child received a total score for all seven words.

First grade tests. All subjects were given the Metropolitan Readiness Test at the beginning of Grade One (Fall 1968).

Second grade tests. The Gates-MacGinitie Reading Test (Primary B) (which yields vocabulary and comprehension scores) was given as a part of the regular school testing program in February of Grade Two (1970). Scores were available for 285 of the original *S*s; scores were not available for the remaining 148 original *S*s. Twenty-nine of the latter *S*s were known to have been retained in Grade one; the remainder had moved, changed schools, or failed to take the test.

The comprehension subtest of the Gates-MacGinitie Reading Test was chosen as a measure of second grade reading performance. *S*s were assigned to one of three groups on the basis of performance on that test: 1) those reading one-half year or more below middle of second grade, 2) those reading three months above or below middle of second grade, and 3) those reading one-half year or more above the middle of second grade. A fourth group consisted of those retained in first grade (N = 29).

Statistical Analysis

Regression Analysis

The effectiveness of the de Hirsch Predictive Index tests for predicting later reading difficulties was assessed in three ways. First, regression analysis was employed to assess the degree of additional information the de Hirsch tests added to the prediction of second grade vocabulary and comprehension scores on the Gates-MacGinitie Reading Test beyond that provided by the use of the Metropolitan Readiness Tests. The relationship of age, sex, and the school attended was added to the equation first. As shown in Tables 1 and 2, the age of the child was not significantly related to either second grade vocabulary or comprehension scores, but the sex of the child (girls predictably did better) and school attended were significantly related to both. (The finding that school attended is significantly related to second grade performance is confounded by differences between the children, differences among the schools, and the fact that different examiners collected data from each of the schools.) Next, scores on each of the Metropolitan Readiness Tests, the total score on the word association test, and each of the de Hirsch Predictive Index Tests were added to the regression equation in that order; and the amount of variance and the additional prediction added by each of these scores were analyzed.

For the mathematically inclined who like to add up degrees of freedom, it should be noted that 17 children were missing one or more of the de Hirsch or Metropolitan test scores and were eliminated from the regression and the discriminate analyses discussed later. Also, only 141 of the 285 children's *Three Bears* stories were scored. *The Three Bears* stories were extremely time consuming to score, and, consequently, a portion of the stories was analyzed before scoring the rest. The partial F ratios, testing the relationship between the number of words used in the *Three Bears* stories and second grade vocabulary and comprehension scores are too small to allow rejection of the hypothesis that the

TABLE 1

SUMMARY OF REGRESSION ANALYSIS USING SECOND GRADE GATES-MACGINITIE COMPREHENSION TEST SCORES AS A CRITERION

Source	df	Total SS	SS Added	F	*p*	MS_e	*R*	S.E. $\hat{Y}$
Age	1	1,577.71	1,577.71	2.53	.25	834.79	.08	28.893
Sex	1	4,160.72	2,583.01	4.15	.05	828.19	.14	28.778
School	5	11,300.15	7,139.43	2.29	.05	816.66	.22	28.577
School × Sex	5	16,188.32	4,888.17	1.57	.25	813.50	.27	28.522
Metropolitan Tests	6	61,219.09	45,030.77	12.04	.0001	652.26	.52	25.539
Word Meaning*	1			1.99	.16			
Listening*	1			1.95	.16			
Matching*	1			0.13	.72			
Alphabet*	1			8.49	.004			
Numbers*	1			1.04	.31			
Copying*	1			0.53	.47			
Total Word Association	1	63,066.98	1,847.89	2.97	.10	647.44	.53	25.445
de Hirsch Tests	10	75,330.01	12,263.03	1.97	.05	623.12	.58	24.962
Bender*	1			0.61	.43			
Gates Word Matching*	1			0.00	.96			
Pencil Use*	1			2.64	.11			
Wepman*				2.09	.15			
X Errors*	1			0.01	.94			
Y Errors*	1			0.45	.50			
Categories*	1			3.52	.06			
Word Reversals*	1			0.87	.35			
Word Recognition I*	1			1.50	.22			
Word Recognition II*	1			8.34	.004			
Word Reproduction*	1							
Residual	238					623.12		

* Note: The values tabled for the individual tests of the Metropolitan and de Hirsch battery are partial *F* ratios—i.e. the relation of that variable to the criterion after the entire model has been fitted.

TABLE 2

SUMMARY OF REGRESSION ANALYSIS USING SECOND GRADE GATES-MACGINITIE VOCABULARY TEST SCORES AS A CRITERION

Source	df	Total SS	SS Added	F	*p*	MS_e	*R*	S.E. $\hat{Y}$
Age	1	865.70		1.50	.25	847.60	.06	29.114
Sex	1	3,285.38	2,392.88	4.15	.05	841.76	.12	29.013
School	5	11,283.16	8,024.58	2.78	.05	827.09	.22	28.759
School × Sex	5	14,332.65	3,049.49	1.06	.50	831.35	.25	28.833
Metropolitan Tests	6	76,720.04	62,387.40	18.04	.0001	600.83	.58	24.512
Word Meaning*	1			1.70	.19			
Listening*	1			2.70	.10			
Matching*	1			.01	.93			
Alphabet*	1			11.37	.0009			
Numbers*	1			3.44	.06			
Copying*	1			3.11	.07			
Total Word Association	1	76,739.89	19.85			603.17	.58	24.560
de Hirsch Tests	10	89,145.03	12,405.14			576.39	.63	24.008
Bender*	1			0.51	.48			
Gates Word Matching*	1			0.61	.44			
Pencil Use*	1			6.57	.01			
Wepman*	1							
X Errors*	1			3.23	.07			
Y Errors*	1			0.43	.51			
Categories*	1			1.15	.28			
Word Reversals*	1			4.24	.04			
Word Recognition I*	1			0.20	.65			
Word Recognition II*	1			0.55	.45			
Word Reproduction*	1			4.37	.04			
Residual	238					576.39		

* Note: The values tabled for the individual tests of the Metropolitan and de Hirsch battery are partial *F* ratios—i.e. the relation of that variable to the criterion after the entire model has been fitted.

Three Bears stories are unrelated to vocabulary and comprehension scores (df = 1,102; F = .81 and .02: $p < .37$ and .88, respectively). Since this variable seemed to be contributing so little prediction, it was dropped from the analysis to avoid contending with missing data. The Metropolitan tests added a highly significant degree of prediction of both second grade vocabulary and comprehension scores (F = 18.04 and 12.04; $p < .0001$). The word-association task added no significant prediction of either score to that allowed by the above variables. Addition of the ten de Hirsch test scores to the regression equation added a slight but significant increase to the prediction of second grade vocabulary (F = 2.15; $p < .025$) and comprehension scores (F = 1.97; $p < .05$).

Analysis of the partial F ratios shown in Tables 1 and 2 reveals the differing effectiveness of the individual subtests of the Metropolitan and the de Hirsch tests for predicting second grade reading performance. The alphabet (letter naming) subtest of the Metropolitan and the word reversals and word reproduction tests of the de Hirsch battery contribute the most to the prediction of second grade comprehension scores. Nearly significant contributions to prediction of comprehension scores are added by the word meaning and listening subtests of the Metropolitan and by the pencil use and auditory discrimination tests of the de Hirsch battery. Individual test variables, significantly related to second grade vocabulary scores as shown by the partial F ratios in Table 2, are the alphabet subtests of the Metropolitan and the pencil use, word reversal, and word reproduction tests of the de Hirsch battery.

Discriminant Analysis

A second statistical strategy employed to compare the predictive effectiveness of the de Hirsch and the Metropolitan Readiness Tests was a test of discriminate analysis. Discriminate analysis allows the assignment of subjects to one of several groups on the basis of statistical similarity to that group. In this case, two groups were employed: the 29 children who were retained in first grade and the remaining subjects who might be identified as passing readers. As mentioned earlier, the two groups could be classified on the basis of their second grade Gates-MacGinitie vocabulary and comprehension scores as either reading at second grade level, or as reading one-half year or more above or below grade level.

If the kindergarten and first grade tests given earlier were effective in predicting later reading achievement, then they should best discriminate those children retained in first grade and those who, although passed to second grade, were still reading below grade level (i.e. children with reading difficulties) from those students reading at least one-half year above grade level (superior readers).

If the tests cannot discriminate between these two extremes of reading performance, then they cannot be expected to discriminate, among students reading more nearly at the average for their grade level. Thus, the attempt was to assign each of the children statistically to either a high risk or to a superior reading group. The fit to the categories actually observed should be best at the two extremes. Assignment of the below average and average readers to either a retained or above average group reflects their statistical similarity to either one or the other of the two groups and should be moderately successful. Thus, if subjects are assigned to one of two groups—poor readers or superior readers—we should be most successful at the extremes and moderately successful with the below average and average second grade readers.

Table 3 indicates that, had the Metropolitan Readiness Test alone been used 28 of the 29 children retained in first grade at the one extreme and 68 of the 79 children who were at the other extreme, i.e. reading one-half year or more above grade level in second grade would have been properly classified. One of the retained students would have been missed and 11 of the above average students would have been misclassified. Knowledge of the de Hirsch test scores in addition to the Metropolitan scores decreases the number of misassignments that we would make in all but the group of children retained in first grade. It should be kept in mind that those assignments were based on kindergarten and first grade readiness tests that had been given nearly two years before.

If our interest is in identifying those children who may experience later reading difficulty, then, by administering the Metropolitan tests, we have decreased the number of high risk children by over half—from 297 to 137. The administration of the de Hirsch tests decrease the original number by two-thirds, from 297 to 98. The success with which the discriminant analysis has assigned nearly all of the retained subjects as well as some of the above average readers to a high risk group indicates that the tests may be difficult for the average kindergarten child. They do pick up most of the failing readers but also a number of the passing readers. Perhaps, as de Hirsch et al. (*1*) observe, ". . . in order to increase the chances of identifying virtually all failing children, it is necessary to throw out a large net, as it were, one which will inevitably pick up some adequate readers."

Still, one is left with the question whether the amount of time required

TABLE 3

THE NUMBER OF SECOND GRADE CHILDREN AT EACH OF FOUR READING LEVELS WHO WERE CLASSIFIED BY DISCRIMINATE ANALYSIS OR AS SUPERIOR READERS ON THE BASIS OF THEIR METROPOLITAN AND DE HIRSCH READINESS TEST SCORES

Dependent Variables	Group Assigned to	Second Grade Gates-MacGinitie Comprehension Performance				
		Retained	Below Grade Level	At Grade Level	Above Grade Level	Total
Metropolitan Readiness Tests only	High Risk	28	43	55	11	137
	Superior	1	35	56	68	160
Metropolitan and de Hirsch Tests	High Risk	27	30	36	5	98
	Superior	2	48	75	74	199
Alphabet Subtest only	High Risk	28	43	55	13	139
	Superior	1	35	56	66	158
Alphabet, Word Reversals and Bender Tests only	High Risk	27	39	38	10	114
	Superior	2	39	73	69	183

to administer the de Hirsch tests, most of which must be administered individually and taking about twenty to thirty minutes per child, is justified by an adequate return on the investment. The clinician's and the teacher's time are valuable commodities. It is reasonable to ask which of the many tests that were given to the children best predict later reading performance.

The same discriminate analysis described was employed to partially answer that question. The program was requested to pick in serial order from all the dependent variables those that best allowed assignment to either a retained or an above average reading group. The best five variables in order of the ability to discriminate later reading ability are the 1) alphabet subtest of the Metropolitan Readiness tests, 2) word reversal, 3) the Bender Visual-Motor Gestalt, 4) word recognition I, and 5) auditory discrimination tests from the de Hirsch battery.

Those tests accounted for most of the variance, and the other tests increased discrimination only slightly. As shown in Table 3, if only the alphabet subtest had been administered, it would have discriminated nearly as well as all six subtests of the Metropolitan Readiness Test. If only the alphabet, word-reversal, and Bender Visual-Motor Gestalt test, had been used, they would have discriminated somewhat better than the total Metropolitan tests and only slightly worse than the Metropolitan and de Hirsch tests combined.

One additional observation should be made. Although both the de Hirsch and Metropolitan tests allow significant prediction of second grade reading scores, the standard error measurement associated with each measure is sufficiently high to preclude very effective prediction of individual cases (cf. Tables 1 and 2). The de Hirsch tests decrease that standard error of measurement only slightly.

Conclusions

The significant prediction of second grade reading performance allowed by the de Hirsch tests given in kindergarten nearly two years before the criterion reading measure points to a developmental consistency that heightens the practical significance for examining these and similar developmental tasks in kindergarten. Thus, the de Hirsch tasks may be useful as tests of developmental skills which should be examined in kindergarten. In addition, they do provide additional prediction of later reading ability beyond that allowed by the Metropolitan tests. It is still questionable, however, whether the time and expense of administering them individually is justified for general testing. They may be very useful, though, in providing additional information for the assessment of marginal kindergarten students, thereby supplementing teacher judgment.

References

1. de Hirsch, Katrina, Jeanette J. Jansky, and William S. Langford. *Predicting Reading Failure: A Preliminary Study*. New York: Harper and Row, 1966.
2. Harris, Albert J. *How to Increase Reading Ability* (5th ed.). New York: McKay, 1970.
3. Strang, Ruth. *Diagnostic Teaching of Reading* (2nd ed.). New York: McGraw-Hill, 1969.

Loisanne P. Bilka
California State College

also reports research on the predictive value of certain tests.

AN EVALUATION OF THE PREDICTIVE VALUE OF CERTAIN READINESS MEASURES

There is some disagreement among educators concerning the value of reading readiness tests. Paradoxicallly, they were developed to solve a problem, not create one. In 1930 Deputy (*4*) reported findings by Percival (1926) and Reed (1927) who conclude that 95-99 percent of school failures are due to failure in reading. Subsequently, Deputy attempted to develop a test to serve as a predictive tool in determining which pupils had the ability necessary to be successful in reading. Standardized reading readiness tests emerged, and their use gained impetus as they won acclaim as reliable measuring instruments. Austin and Morrison (*1*) report that more than 80 percent of the 940 school systems which participated in the questionnaire survey of the Harvard Report used readiness tests to help determine when children should begin instruction in a formal reading program.

With the passage of time, many research investigations have been conducted, and points of view concerning readiness and readiness tests have changed. The concept of readiness has evolved from earlier beliefs that maturation is all that is necessary for reading success to more recent concepts that reading readiness can be developed and that the interaction of nature and nurture is essential for learning.

Purposes of the Study

The present study was undertaken to offer further data about the predictive value of reading readiness tests. The two purposes of this study were to ascertain if reading achievement in grades one, two, and three can be predicted by certain standardized reading readiness and intelligence measures and to determine if their predictive ability is significantly related to method of instruction, sex differences, or mental age.

The following hypotheses were tested in this investigation: 1) that there is no significant relationship between intelligence, reading readiness test measures, and reading achievement; 2) that there is no significant relationship between the subtests within each readiness test (Murphy-Durrell and Metropolitan) and reading achievement; 3) that there is no significant relationship between the major contributing subtests of the various measuring instruments, in different combinations, used in this study and reading achievement; 4) that there is no significant difference in the predictive ability of reading achievement from readiness measures when comparing grade one predictors to grade one achievement, to grade two achievement, and to grade three achievement; and 5) that the ability of a test to predict reading achievement is not significantly reflective of the method of reading instruction used or by the organismic factors of sex and mental age and that there is not interaction between these organismic factors and the method factor.

Design of Study

The sample population, consisting of 353 Pittsburgh public school children, was randomly assigned to 18 classrooms. Nine of these classes were instructed through the coordinated language arts materials of Scott, Foresman basal approach while the other nine used a language arts program that integrated language experience with individualized reading (the integrated experience approach to communication developed at the University of Pittsburgh).

Readiness measures were administered to the children at the beginning of first grade. They were the Banham Checklist—Maturity Level for School Entrance, 1960; Metropolitan Readiness Test, Form A, 1964; Murphy-Durrell Diagnostic Reading Readiness Test, revised edition, 1964; Thurstone Jeffrey Identical Forms and Pattern Copying Tests, 1964; and the intelligence measure of the Pintner-Cunningham Primary Test, Form A, 1964. The appropriate Stanford Achievement Test was given to the same sample in May of first grade, May of second grade, and May of third grade.

Fifty-three teachers participated in the investigation. The teachers were assigned to each classroom by the principal of each participating school. The teachers received supervision through preservice and monthly workshops.

Statistical Analysis of Data

Specific statistical techniques of canonical correlation, 2 × 2 × 2 factorial analysis of variance, and Hotelling's *t* test of significance of differences were applied to the data.

The first three hypotheses were tested by the use of the canonical correlation model. Originally developed by Hotelling in 1936 and described by Cooley and Lohnes (*3*), this method determines the relationships between linear functions of multiple predictor variables (the various readiness measures and intelligence measures) and multiple criterion variables (four subtests of the Stanford Reading Achievement Test). Geometrically, the canonical model can be considered to be an exploration of the extent to which individuals occupy the same relative position in one test space as they do in the other. In addition to canonical correlations determined, the factor structure of each significant linear function is revealed to show which variables contribute most heavily to the maximally correlated components. Chi-square tests of significance were applied to determine the significance of correlations.

Hotelling's *t* test was used to test the fourth hypothesis regarding the correlated data, while the fifth hypothesis was tested through the use of a 2 × 2 × 2 multivariate factorial analysis of variance.

Findings

Hypothesis 1

To comply with the restrictions of the canonical model, that variables must not be linearly related, the six readiness variables were analyzed in two sets. Set 1 consisted of the Murphy-Durrell Reading Readiness total score, Thurstone Pattern Copying Test and the Thurstone Identical Forms Test. Set 2 included the Banham Test of Social Maturity, Metropolitan Readiness Test, and the Pintner-Cunningham Intelligence Test.

Canonical correlations applied to total test scores revealed significant relationships (at the .001 level) between the predictor variables and criterion variables of reading achievement at each grade level (set one .63, .64, and .60 for grades one, two, and three, respectively; and set two .56, .53, and .54 in grades one, two, and three, respectively). The factor loadings indicated that the Murphy-Durrell Readiness Test and the Metropolitan Readiness Tests were the strongest contributors to prediction (.98 and .97 factor loadings at grade one, .97 and .92 at grade two, and .96 and .97 at grade three).

Hypothesis 2

This hypothesis was concerned only with tests made up of various subtests, namely the Murphy-Durrell Reading Readiness Analysis Test and the Metropolitan Reading Readiness Test. Highly significant correlations (.001 level) were found between the predictor variables and the domain of reading achievement when results of both tests were examined.

It was found that all three subtests of the Murphy-Durrell contributed significantly to the predictor domain. The phonemes subtest was the strongest contributor in grades one and two (factor loadings of .86 and .84, respectively) while total letter names was strongest in grade 3 (factor loading of .82). All subtests displayed factor loadings of .60 or higher at each grade level.

Three of the subtests of the Metropolitan (word meaning, numbers, and alphabet) exhibited factor loadings of .60 or higher at all three grade levels. Word meaning was the strongest contributor at grade 1 (factor loading of .81) while the alphabet subtest was strongest at grade two and grade three (.79 and .75, respectively). The other subtests —listening, copying, and matching—did not display factor loadings above .50 at any time.

Hypothesis 3

In order to test this hypothesis, the canonical-correlation technique was applied to ten different combinations of subtests of both of the predictor measuring instruments (Murphy-Durrell and Metropolitan) and the criterion variables of reading achievement. Each test used in these recombinations gave previous evidence of a factor loading of .60 or higher in the statistical analysis of hypothesis one and two. Prior to recombination analyses, correlations ranged from .30 to .63. Correlations in recombination analyses changed in range from .55 to .67. The highest correlation of .67 was found using the phonemes, letter names, and learning rate subtests of the Murphy-Durrell, plus the Metropolitan word meaning subtest.

Hypothesis 4

Tests of significance showed correlations did not drop significantly from grade to grade despite a downward trend. Therefore, the ability to predict third grade reading achievement by means of readiness tests was almost as accurate as prediction of first grade reading achievement.

Hypothesis 5

The $2 \times 2 \times 2$ multivariate analysis of variance determined that the factors of sex, mental age, and method of instruction do influence the ability of the Murphy-Durrell Test to predict reading achievement accurately at the first grade level. Mental age and method remained significant factors at the second grade level while none were significant at the third grade level.

Tests of significance applied to the mean scores of the Metropolitan Test indicated the same pattern as with the Murphy-Durrell for the first two years. At the third grade level, however, the effects of sex and mental age on the predictive value of the Metropolitan Test were also significant.

On the basis of these multivariate scores (that is, taking into account all variables) over the three-year period, it is evident that the factors of sex, mental age, and method do influence ability to predict reading achievement.

An examination of cell means and univariate F tests revealed that the Murphy-Durrell Test is abler in predicting boys' achievement than girls'; is more accurate for high mental-age students (6.5 years or higher) than for those of low mental age; and is a better predictor for children taught with the basal approach.

A similar examination revealed the Metropolitan to be a more accurate predictor for girls than boys; for high mental-age children in comparison to those of low mental age; and for children taught through the basal approach in comparison to children taught through the integrated experiences approach.

Conclusions

As a result of these findings one can conclude:

1. Of the tests examined, the Murphy-Durrell Reading Readiness Test demonstrates the strongest and highest relationship to reading achievement measured by the Stanford Achievement Test. In addition, it is least influenced by sex differences.
2. The Metropolitan Readiness Test is the second best predictive instrument of those examined; however, the subtests of matching, copying, and listening contribute little to predicting reading success. In an effort to save teacher-pupil time in administration and scoring, it is suggested that these subtests should not be given. Sex differences also strongly influence the predictive ability of this test.
3. The Pintner-Cunningham Primary Test makes a moderate con-

tribution to the domain of prediction. The factor loadings weaken over the time period, indicating that its predictive ability may not be so stable as in the other tests measured.

4. The Banham Checklist—Maturity Level for School Entrance; Thurstone Jeffrey Identical Forms Test, and Pattern Copying Tests are not so adequate predictors as the Murphy-Durrell or Metropolitan Readiness Test.
5. When unique subtests of the Murphy-Durrell and Metropolitan tests are combined, the strongest relationship between the prediction and achievement domain is obtained by combining the word meaning subtest of the Metropolitan with the three subtests of the Murphy-Durrell. The correlation remains relatively stable over the primary years.
6. Phonemes and letter names subtests in combination are strong predictors and give verification to Durrell's research that these are *the* two most important factors for predicting reading success. The combination also reemphasizes the importance of developing skills of visual and auditory perception and discrimination.
7. No significant differences were found when *t* tests were applied between the readiness measures and achievement in each grade level, indicating third grade success can be predicted as well as first.
8. The school administrator should consider the materials to be used in instruction when choosing tests because the tests examined in this study predicted better for children who were taught through the basal reader approach.
9. There is a general trend for both the Murphy-Durrell and the Metropolitan tests to be more accurate predictors for children with mental ages of 6.5 years or older.

References

1. Austin, Mary C., and Coleman Morrison. *The First R: The Harvard Report on Reading in the Elementary School.* New York: Macmillan, 1963.

2. Bremer, Neville. "Do Readiness Tests Predict Success in Reading?" *Elementary School Journal,* 59 (January 1959), 222-224.

3. Cooley, William W., and Paul R. Lohnes. *Multivariate Procedures for the Behavioral Sciences.* New York: John Wiley and Sons, 1962.

4. Deputy, Erby Chester. "Predicting First Grade Reading Achievement," *Contributions to Education #426.* New York: Columbia University, 1930.

5. Karlin, Robert. "The Prediction of Reading Success and Reading Readiness Tests," *Elementary English,* 34 (May 1957), 320-322.

IS IT "BEST" TO TEACH READING TO PRESCHOOLERS?

Lloyd O. Ollila
University of Victoria

finds some answers and opinions and presents some conclusions.

PROS AND CONS OF TEACHING READING TO FOUR- AND FIVE-YEAR-OLDS

The teaching of reading to four- and five-year-olds (and even those younger as suggested in *How to Teach Your Baby to Read* (*5*), has been a long and hotly debated topic among educators and a source of anxiety to parents. Traditionally, the elementary school curriculum has set the beginning of reading instruction at grade one—in deference to the popular idea that six is the age when most children can successfully learn to read and since some school systems have no kindergartens. From the late fifties and early sixties a number of experiments (*3, 6, 7, 12*) demonstrate that some children can successfully learn to read at ages five, four, and even three and two. These studies, popularized in magazines and newspapers, were combined with the child development movement away from leaving all to maturation and toward nurturing learning abilities instead.

As a result, pressure from both educators and parents to begin reading at earlier ages was felt. Opponents and advocates of early reading took sides, and there was a surge of research on such topics as reading in the kindergarten and characteristics of early readers.

The trend of bringing youngsters to reading at younger ages has clearly arrived and can be easily seen in the profusion of parent-teach-your-preschooler-books and workbooks, the bandwagon of readiness programs, and even the conscious orientation of children's television programs such as *Sesame Street* toward teaching letters and word families to preschoolers. Today the controversy over early reading has changed focus from the question, "Can children under six years of age learn to read?" to the following questions: "Why should they read earlier?" "What are the benefits of reading early?" and "To whom should early reading instruction be given?" These questions should be raised seriously now that the trend to early reading is gaining momentum.

Why Preschoolers and Kindergartners Should Learn to Read

Advocates feel that, nowadays, more children are ready for reading activities at an earlier age than used to be the case. They maintain that children today have changed in many ways and are involved in more varied activities than their counterparts of pre-World War II days. They (*3, 8, 13*) point to studies showing today's children's greater vocabularies, to the explosion in communication industries, and to greater mobility which provides many children with more and varied experiences, including greater exposure to the printed word. They also emphasize the growing number of children who attend nursery school and other preschool programs which, they maintain, are not unlike traditional kindergarten.

While children have changed in the past 15 to 20 years, they contend that the kindergartens of today have remained relatively static. Supporters of early reading argue that kindergartens should reevaluate their curricula, adjust to individual differences, and provide "suitable" activities, including reading for the child of today. They believe that many kindergarten children are ready and eager to read and would profit from instruction. They feel that past practices have ignored the instructional needs of children who come to kindergarten able to read books. The preschooler who comes to kindergarten able to read books has to await the end of the first grade reading readiness period before the teacher lets him read his first preprimer.

Why Children Shouldn't Learn to Read Early

Many of the opponents and others with reservations (*1, 10*) about early reading would agree that the kindergarten child today should be treated differently from his counterparts of 15 to 20 years ago, but agreement ends on whether early reading is one of the areas to alter. Possibly this view is best summed up by the question, "Is reading instruction the best use to make of the ages of three, four, and five?" There is the fear that too much emphasis on early reading may lead to a less rounded development of the child because skills in the social and sensory-motor areas will receive less attention. Instead, it is argued that the emphasis at this age should involve a more horizontal approach—a development of a solid foundation of experiences, a broadening of these experiences, a consolidation of learnings—as an insurance that almost all children would be ready for reading activities. For instance, Ames (*1*), director of research at the Gesell Institute of Child Development, contends that a delay in reading instruction would be a preventative measure in avoiding nearly all reading failure. She feels that children who are pushed into reading too soon may never read as well as they would have, had instruction been delayed. Instead of early reading she recommends giving children richer and more varied experiences.

Effects of Early Reading

Claims of benefits and counterclaims of harmful consequences abound in the literature. Facts to substantiate each claim are few and can be seen in the following discussion of four such claims.

1. *Children who get an early start in reading will have only a temporary advantage over children who begin reading in first grade.* Although Vernon's study (*18*) of early readers in England and Scotland found that their initial advantages in reading achievement were not necessarily maintained in the intermediate grades, more recent investigations indicate that the early starter does maintain his lead. Durkin's longitudinal studies (*8*) of preschool readers report higher achievement over equally bright nonearly readers—even when instruction was not adjusted to the abilities of some of the early readers. In a study of kindergarten instruction in reading, Sutton (*16*) offers a program of beginning reading instruction the second semester of kindergarten with a total of "not more than 20 hours' kindergarten time." She also found the early readers maintaining higher reading scores at the end of third grade.

Brezeinski's study (*3*) of early reading involving 4,000 children is of special interest. The Denver public schools taught beginning reading to selected kindergarten groups. On entrance to first grade, those groups were divided and placed either in a traditional or an adjusted instructional program. By the fifth grade, it was found that early readers who had the adjusted instruction scored significantly higher on tests of reading vocabulary, comprehension, rate, and study skills than did their counterparts who began reading in first grade. However, the early readers who were put into traditional programs without the adjusted instruction lost their early advantage and scored similarly to those who began reading in first grade.

One frequent criticism of research in early reading is that findings are often based on a selective sample of highly advantaged bright children. The Denver study (*3*), however, included below average children. Durkin's study (7) included children with IQs as low as 91. Bereiter's study (*2*) of teaching reading to four-year-olds of different socioeconomic backgrounds reports that lower class children could be brought to the 1.1 level by the first year and to the 2.6 grade level by the end of the third year.

As research has shown that many different types of kindergartners can profit from early reading, Durkin (*7*) speculates that slow learners might especially benefit from an early start. She reasons that the longer periods of time involved would allow for more gradual introduction of reading activities suitable to the slower child's learning rate.

2. *Early readers will have better attitudes toward reading.* That many advocates see some of the benefits of early reading in terms of a better attitude toward reading and a greater interest in books may be inferred from the following remarks gathered from the literature: "Pupils were described by their teachers as 'book hungry' " (*16*); "Children should be taught to read as early as possible because this is one of the few keys to building a lifelong desire to read" (*13*); and "A kindergartner wants to learn to read. . . . He'll never be better motivated" (*17*). Considering its importance, this topic, surprisingly, has received little research interest, and the few studies considering it do so only as a side effect of their main study.

Brezeinski (*3*), using the quantity of independent reading as an index of enjoyment and interest in reading, reports that an early or accelerated reading program enhanced interest in reading for a period of several years (second, third, and fourth grades), but by the fifth grade this lead disappeared and no significant differences were apparent. In Kelley's experiment cited by Downing (*6*), children's end-of-the-year attitudes toward kindergarten reading were measured on a self-reporting inventory. Kelley first devised a pilot program in which children in an experimental kindergarten group could choose whether they wanted to be given reading instruction. Preliminary evaluation revealed that, by the second grade, the early kindergarten readers were not only significantly advanced in reading skills but also more positive in their attitudes toward reading. However, when Kelley set up a full scale scientific research, the experimental group included both those who wished to read and those that did not. It was then found that the control group who had no kindergarten reading had more favorable attitudes.

3. *Early reading is harmful to a child's eyesight.* Curiously, although this is one of the oldest and most commonly voiced arguments against

early reading, few facts are really known today. Holmes (*9*), in a summary of the research on visual hazards in early reading, states, "There is little experimental evidence dealing with changes in children's eyes between the ages of two and five with or without the imposition of the task of learning to read." He points out that there seems to be little evidence to support theories that teaching reading after age four leads to increase in myopia (nearsightedness). A survey of the several longitudinal studies of preschool and kindergarten readers (*3, 7, 16*) shows that none of the reported significant differences between early readers and later starters was in the number of sight defects.

4. *Early reading will result in psychological and social problems.* Teaching children to read early results in too much pressure, boredom, confusion, frustration, more reading problems, and psychosocial maladjustment—some of the many predictions of dire consequences resulting from teaching three-, four-, and five-year-olds to read. That these outcomes are mostly supported by well-publicized personal opinions is shown in a search through the number of investigations that deal with the issue. In the six-year study of early reading in the Denver schools, Brezeinski (*3*) found that early reading neither created problems nor prevented the problems of reading disabilities and harmful social and psychological effects. Other investigations (*7, 16*) reached similar conclusions.

Problems in the Kindergarten

Many of the criticisms of teaching reading early seem centered not so much on the question of "should children read early" but on kindergarten teachers' competencies for teaching reading, problems of organizing reading instruction in kindergarten, and current reading programs. Several recent surveys (*4, 11*) would suggest that many kindergarten teachers do not have the necessary training to give reading instruction. Ching (*4*) found that there are wide differences in reading preparation as measured by number of college reading courses taken, ranging from 0-32 in a sample of 931 California kindergarten teachers. Furthermore, school systems interested in adopting early reading may meet resistance from some teachers. One survey (*11*) of 500 teachers found that many teachers believed that "the few who are ready to read comprise so small a minority that it is not worth revising the present kindergarten program."

A second problem revolves around the degree to which the kindergarten can practically and effectively organize reading instruction that will meet the needs of each child. Downing (*6*), who reports successful experiments with early readers in Great Britain, maintains "the younger the pupils, the greater the need for an individual approach." The current kindergarten picture with a high pupil-teacher ratio, a wide range of differences in readiness and experience, and short class time is seen as adding to the difficulty of organizing reading programs that not only fit the situation but also fit the needs of the child. Two surveys of current kindergarten programs (*4, 11*) report that a common practice gaining momentum in kindergartens is the mass instruction approach in which all the kindergartners in the class are taught together in the same reading program. Both advocates and opponents of early reading have expressed doubts whether all children in any one kindergarten class could profit from the same early reading instruction given at the same pace.

Many critics are skeptical of the way the concept of early reading has been translated into classroom practices. Discussing visits to kindergarten classrooms where reading was being taught, Hymes (*10*) and Sheldon (*14*) express deep concerns over the serious no-nonsense atmosphere, the silent passive learning, the pencil-pushing activities, and the irrelevant materials which all too frequently characterize the programs. Critics also argue that some current kindergarten reading programs are actually poorly diluted copies of the first grade reading program without adequate adjustments for kindergarten differences.

If, perhaps, there is some truth to these arguments, these abuses could be partly accounted for by the fact that teachers have few guidelines on what materials, methods, and general procedures might be effectively used. Research studies comparing different programs constantly find contradictory results. Little research has been given to the possibility that some methods and materials will be more suitable for certain kindergarten children than for others.

Conclusions

The whole issue of early reading remains unresolved, and for many it is clouded in emotional appeals, extreme claims, and misunderstandings of terminology. Opponents have used such negative emotional appeals as "being cheated out of childhood" and "pushed into learning." While these comments make lively reading, they also help to block intelligent discussion. In the same vein, the extremes of the argument—"all children should begin reading early" and "no child should read early" should not be generalized nor accepted as the view of the majority of both opponents and advocates. Most people concerned with early reading fall well between the polar extremes and attach certain conditions to their arguments.

Further misunderstanding occurs, as Smith (*15*) observes, through different conceptions of terminology. What does a writer mean when he argues that young children should be taught to read early? How "early"? By "reading" does he mean, mainly, teaching word analysis skills or does he include teaching sight vocabulary and comprehension skills? What does he mean by "teaching"? It is interesting to speculate how the issue of early reading would become more manageable without the emotional appeals and extremes and if each writer would explain his conception of the terminology.

Clearly, the pros and cons of early reading will not be resolved until more facts are known. Too much time and effort have been wasted on opinions of what may happen and on reaction to those opinions. There actually is little research (although what there is has been widely publicized) to substantiate claims of the effects of early reading. Of the research available, it can tentatively be said:

1. Most studies lend support to the claim that children who have an early start in reading will exhibit higher reading achievement than their later-starting counterparts and will maintain this advantage, especially if adjusted instruction is provided. This finding underlines the importance that school systems, interested in implementing early reading programs, realize a total commitment—not merely a change in the kindergarten program but necessary changes adjusting instruction in other grades as well.
2. There is an indication that attitudes of kindergartners toward reading may be partly related to the teacher's selection of children to participate in the early reading program. In two studies (*6, 16*) where kindergarten children could choose whether they wanted to join the reading program, the children seemed to enjoy reading more than their counterparts. Perhaps, for those children who are not interested in reading, the teacher should spend more time "selling" them on books and building motivation so they will be more eager to read at a later time.
3. So little is known about the effects of early reading on eyesight that even the most enthusiastic advocates should take cautious note.

4. Early reading seems neither to create nor prevent reading disabilities, problems of boredom, school adjustment, or psychological problems. These problems, however, can be attributed to poor teaching and inappropriate methods and materials used in instruction. Advocates of early reading should feel a pressing need to provide better guidelines grounded in research about different organizational plans, reading approaches, methods, materials, and their suitability for different kindergarten children. If better guidelines are not provided, it seems likely that some questionable current practices will continue, and critics will find their evidence of harmful effects.

References

1. Ames, Louise B. "A Developmental Approach to Reading Problems," paper presented at the Claremont Reading Conference, Claremont, California, 1966.

2. Bereiter, Carl. "Instruction of Three- and Four-Year-Old Children," *Child Study,* 29 (Fall and Winter 1967), 3-11.

3. Brzeinski, Joseph B. *Summary Report of the Effectiveness of Teaching Reading in the Denver Public Schools,* Cooperative Research Project No. 5-0371. Denver, Colorado: Denver Public Schools.

4. Ching, Doris. "The Teaching of Reading in Kindergarten," paper presented at the International Reading Association Convention, Anaheim, California, 1970.

5. Doman, Glen. *How to Teach Your Baby to Read.* New York: Random House, 1964.

6. Downing, John, and Derek Thackray. *Reading Readiness.* London: University of London Press, 1971.

7. Durkin, Dolores. "Earlier Start in Reading?" *Elementary School Journal,* 63 (December 1962), 146-151.

8. Durkin, Dolores. "When Should Children Begin to Read?" *Sixty Seventh Yearbook of the National Society for the Study of Education, Part II.* Chicago: University of Chicago Press, 1968, 30-71.

9. Holmes, Jack. "Visual Hazards in the Early Teaching of Reading," in H. K. Smith (Ed.), *Perception and Reading.* Newark, Delaware: International Reading Association, 1968, 53-61.

10. Hymes, James L. "Teaching Reading to the Under-Six Age: A Child

Development Point of View," paper presented at the Claremont Reading Conference, Claremont, California, 1970.

11. LaConte, Christine. "Reading in the Kindergarten: Fact or Fantasy?" *Elementary English,* 47 (March 1970), 382-387.

12. Moore, Omar K. "Orthographic Symbols and the Preschool Child—A New Approach," unpublished paper, Sociology Department, Yale University, 1959.

13. Newman, Robert E. "The Kindergarten Reading Controversy," *Elementary English,* 43 (March 1966), 235-239.

14. Sheldon, William D. "A Modern Reading Program for Young Children," in W. G. Cutts (Ed.), *Teaching Young Children to Read.* Washington: United States Department of Health, Education, and Welfare, Office of Education Bulletin 1964, No. 19, 31-37.

15. Smith, Nila Banton. "Perspectives: Teaching Young Children to Read," in A. Beery et al (Eds.), *Elementary Reading Instruction.* Boston: Allyn and Bacon, 1969, 339-347.

16. Sutton, Marjorie H. "Children Who Learned to Read in Kindergarten: A Longitudinal Study," *Reading Teacher,* 22 (April 1969), 595-602, 683.

17. "To Read or Not to Read in Kindergarten?" *Grade Teacher,* May-June 1968, 153-155.

18. Vernon, P. E., M. B. O'Gorman, and T. McClellan. "Comparative Study of Educational Attainments in England and Scotland," *British Journal of Educational Psychology,* 25 (November 1955), 195-203.

WHAT STRATEGIES ARE "BEST" IN PRESCHOOL BEGINNING READING PROGRAMS?

Joseph E. Brzeinski and Gerald E. Elledge
Denver, Colorado, Schools

present some answers obtained from experience with the two Denver studies.

EARLY READING*

The saga of early childhood reading is somewhat reminiscent of the radio soap opera of yesteryear: the characters lived on and on; the progress was almost predictable; and should one have neglected to listen for a month or a year, not too much in the plot would have been missed.

In our continuing story, the program producers continue to use the theories and guidelines of Bloom, Bruner, Deutsch, Fowler, Hebb, Hunt, Piaget, and others. The success and potential of early childhood reading have been reported again and again. Research evidence regarding adverse effects of early reading instruction is lacking and almost nonexistent although reading research and instruction have been the topics of over twenty-five thousand articles and publications. Many of the shibboleths existing ten years ago have been discredited. Yet the same tired voices continue to warn against early reading instruction.

However, the story is changing. Professional and public recognition of the values of early intervention are having an influence. The federally supported Education Acts of 1965 accelerated innovation. Head Start and *Sesame Street* have dramatically highlighted the plot of our continuing story. Still in many communities both effective early childhood education and early reading instruction are strongly theoretical and exist mainly within limited special programs and, consequently, serve the few rather than provide such educational opportunities to the majority of young children.

The inadequacy of research applied to improving reading instruction has been highlighted for those seeking to implement the "Right to Read—Target for the 70s." The writings of Chall, Durkin, Cohen, Robinson,

* Portions of this article appeared in the December 1971 issue of *The Reading Teacher.*

Smith, and others, and the current United States Office of Education "Targeted Program in Reading" are indicants that the basic quest remains unfulfilled—namely, that *every* child will attain reading competence to meet both his individual needs and those of urban, technical, industrialized culture within a democratic and humanized matrix. That would seem to be a reasonable goal, yet the complexity of it is indicated by David Dempsey who notes in a recent article in the *Saturday Review*, "Paradoxically, as the educational level of the country has risen, so has the rate of functional illiteracy. For this condition, one logically blames the schools; yet, the problem is not so simple. As American industry makes increasingly sophisticated demands upon even its lowest paid workers, standards of literacy rise, too."

Historical Perspective

The documentation of the need to read has been evident for over seven thousand years. Ever since man first began to record his ideas in writing, this need has been persistent; and its fulfillment has been of high priority. The elite—those who could read at the court of Hammurabi, the scribes of ancient Egypt, the scholars of Oriental lands, and elsewhere—all possessed the rare and valuable skills of reading.

Our society formalized reading instruction requirements when, in 1642, the general court of Massachusetts declared that parents and masters were responsible for the development of reading skills among their children. The court further required that respect for laws and religion would be taught all children. From this meager beginning, we have, through a system of mass education operating with significant resource limitations, a national illiteracy rate of less than 2 percent. Admittedly, one of four pupils nationwide is said to have significant reading difficulties. In a sense, these are the persistent characteristics of statistical interpretations as related to normative classifications of data. Similar statistical data would apply to most of the learned skills.

Viewed from the perspective of history, reading ability—the skill of the elite—has become a common skill, possessed to a degree by over 98 percent of our citizenry. Yet, complacency about the seriousness of the reading problem is not permissible, for as Walter Straley of the National Reading Council notes, "As many as 18.5 million Americans, or 13 percent of the population 16 years and older, lack the reading ability necessary for survival in the United States today." The answer to the problem lies somewhere between what has already been done, what is currently being recognized as effective early reading instruction, and a synthesis of these elements into a functional implementation process.

During the 1960s, we witnessed a technological revolution but, as yet, have failed to use this technology to implement the techniques with proven validity. The restricted size of our research samples and the lack of significant home-parent involvement have predetermined ineffectiveness or at best only partial success.

If educational research in early childhood education is to have a major impact, it must include the added dimension of the home. Thus, we recognize a multipronged thrust: the home fulfilling a preventive role; the school providing identification and programs for recognized, modifiable deficiencies; and research-evaluating processes and procedures. In order to attain these ends, we must clearly define the nature of the variations among children and the processes by which the learning of reading takes place.

Researchers suggest that we must reorder our educational priorities; we must give additional emphasis to early childhood education. The dividend potential of early preschool education has been reiterated by numerous investigators: Fowler (*9*), Cicarelli et al (*3*), Weikart, along with Deutsch (*5*), and Bloom et al (*2*), most of whom have focused attention on the effects of cultural deprivation and potential approaches to remediating its consequences.

Early Development of the Learner

Bloom (*1*) observes that from the time of conception until age eight, 80 percent of intelligence is developed, and there remains little doubt that this development is, in part, a function of the environment in which the individual operates. That is a time of plasticity, when the impact of instruction may have its greatest influence. The years four to eight, then, are crucial in the development of the cognitive skills for reading.

A factor having great impact in support of early reading instruction is Bloom's hypothesis (*1*): "Variations in the environment have greatest quantitative effect on a characteristic at its most rapid period of change and least effect on a characteristic during the least rapid period of change." In a similar view, Hunt suggests there is a need to pay more attention to the early years, and particularly so if there is evidence of cultural deprivation. He also stresses the importance of the "match," meaning the junction between the external stimuli and the inner integrative pattern of the individual. Experiential deprivation and/or ineffective or inappropriate instruction can be harmful to students at any age.

Hebb, along with others, indicates that early experience is crucial for proper development of problem-solving and interest in the environment. There seems to be an intrinsic pleasure or self reward in gaining confidence that feeds upon itself and leads to further development.

Primary learning in humans is a perceptual experience; man is dependent upon visual and visual-motor processing for adequate development. To deprive the infant or child of visual, motor, and kinaesthetic experiences contributes to perceptual dysfunctioning.

Behavioral changes can be achieved more easily at an early age. The adaptive, useful behaviors are established very early in the child's life. The maladaptive behaviors are just as easily acquired. We can no longer afford the luxury of investigating whether the child can be taught at an early age; the research evidence is rather conclusive in this regard. The child is not waiting; he is learning, be it in a positive or negative direction. The questions remaining are "What to teach him?" and "How to teach him?"

Reading Skill and the Preschool Child

The readiness doctrine, which imposes an age-six chronological barrier to formal learning, sentences many children to failure and ignores the learning abilities of others. The literature on gifted children contains reports of children who have mastered the alphabet during the second year or have begun reading text as early as the third year. As has been widely reported, Omar K. Moore has succeeded, with the aid of the responsive environment typewriter, to teach children as young as three years of age to read. Fowler (*9*) reports substantial headway in teaching more than 80 four-year-olds and 15 three-year-olds to read fluently.

Indications are that success in early reading is rather consistently found to be at a minimal mental age criterion of about four years. Because of national demands and to help solve the problem of Oriental immigrants, Israel has organized free nursery schools where four-year-old children are introduced to reading. For a long time in selected schools in the Soviet Union, Scotland, and the Montesorri Schools of Europe children have been taught to read between the age of four and six.

Durkin (*7*), working in Oakland, California, found that almost 1 percent of pupils entering first grade scored between 1.5 and 4.5 on a grade level norm scale in reading. In 40 New York schools, she found that 157 pupils, or almost 4 percent, entered first grade as readers.

The Exemplary Center for Reading Instruction (ECRI) in Utah reports results indicating that preschool reading instruction is effective and that those who entered the program at age three are doing the best. Cohen (*4*), as a result of his work with disadvantaged children, concludes that we must discard the old shibboleth that reading instruction in preschool is injurious to children.

Head Start and other programs to equalize educational opportunities demand the intervention and stimulation of early childhood education to prepare the child to benefit from school—early education which, incidentally, is a reading environment.

Television, specifically *Sesame Street,* reaches six million or about one-half of the population three to five years of age; and the research indicates that those who watch regularly do learn letters, numbers, and object-matching skills. More important, perhaps, are the overt reading-related behaviors exhibited by toddlers in their livingrooms, behaviors they will bring to school.

The Denver Studies

Reading skills can be learned by the child prior to his customary entrance in school. Two benchmark studies (*15*) demonstrate that a large urban public school system can significantly upgrade reading achievement. One study provided reading instruction to large numbers of typical kindergarten pupils; the other study utilized the medium of television to assist parents in preparing their preschool children for learning. That television study has been replicated by Schoephoerster (*20*) and McManus (*16*), both of whom reaffirm the value of parents' preparing their young children for reading. In a corollary-type study, Dunn (*6*), demonstrates that children, two to four years of age, can be effectively taught selected reading skills by use of the television medium.

Essentially, the Denver television study utilized a series of 16 television lessons and accompanying guidebooks to assist preschool children, with parental guidance, to acquire basic skills of beginning reading. Participants had a minimum chronological age of at least four and one-half years (54 months).

Results reveal that statistically significant gains in achievement were made by those children who practice 30 minutes or more per week. The amount a child learned depended directly on the length of time someone practiced the beginning reading activities with him. (The favorable findings more recently related to *Sesame Street* were of no surprise to the educators in Denver.)

The Denver kindergarten study found that beginning reading skills can be taught quite effectively to typical kindergarten pupils; large numbers of pupils were involved within a conventional kindergarten structure. Follow-up studies indicate that the permanence of gains made, as a result of being taught beginning reading in kindergarten, depend upon subsequent instruction.

Head Start administrators also have come to recognize the significance of subsequent instruction; and, as a result, various follow-through programs have been developed to capitalize upon and to sustain the gains of early childhood education made by Head Start.

Reading comprehension and reading vocabulary results were high among the experimental groups in Denver; those groups were also comprised of faster readers. Subsequent analysis established that earlier reading influenced achievement in other areas where success depended upon reading proficiency. The experimental instruction, both during kindergarten and in the later grades, proved to be more effective than the regular reading program used previously. The early reading program presented no blocks, physical or emotional, to later reading.

Learning to read is very similar to mastering speech; if the child is capable of acquiring a differential speech response to ordinary stimuli in a normal manner, then the same thing is true of reading. Thus, learning to *see* words is closely parallel to learning to *hear* words. The difficulties we experience in teaching reading may well stem primarily from the method of exposure and the quality of instruction rather than the maturational level or limitation in the child as a learner.

A questionnaire survey conducted by Zaruba (*23*) found that most kindergarten and primary teachers have positive attitudes toward including reading instruction in kindergarten. Noteworthy is the fact that primary teachers attributed greater importance than kindergarten teachers to the more formal reading skills and to parental involvement. A two-state survey by LaConte (*13*) reports that resistance to teaching reading in kindergarten apparently is related to length of teaching experience. Teachers in large cities, however, were more strongly in favor of early reading instruction than those in other areas.

Results from the Comparative Reading Approach First Grade Teaching (CRAFT) (*18*) indicate that the type of experience provided Negro disadvantaged children in the New York public school kindergartens appeared to be beneficial for only those who had subsequent reading instruction in a language-experience program. Largest gains were made in grade three, indicating delayed effects from this approach.

Langston (*14*), Karnes (*11*), Kelley and Chen (*12*), and Sutton (*22*) have all found significantly higher achievement among experimental groups who received early instruction in comparison with control groups. The kindergarten and early childhood program should be more than permissive play. The play experiences designed to promote personal and social development should be accompanied by content and structured activities to improve the intellectual climate during this crucial time of a child's life.

The increased cultural advantages of our relatively affluent society, improved materials for instruction, and recognized changes which have occurred in the environment of children suggest that youngsters may develop an aptitude for reading at an earlier age than previously has been the case.

The Role of the Home

Within the average home young children deal more easily with the big ideas of their environment and, as a result, have speaking vocabularies that are probably close to five thousand words, with listening vocabularies twice the size of their speaking vocabularies. They ask big questions and expect correct and detailed answers.

Preprimary children in many homes are surrounded with reading materials of many types which are used for varied purposes by all members of the families; at an early age the children learn to know the importance of such materials. Youngsters read familiar street signs, assist in warning the driver of the family car of traffic signs, and help mothers hunt the attractively packaged and familiar products in stores. They note the eye-catching printed materials that arrive through the mail and are subtly influenced by television commercials.

The Gallup Studies of Early Childhood Learning (*8*), through interviews with mothers, established support for early reading instruction. In addition, it was found that most of the top first grade pupils had been read to regularly at home before they entered first grade, that the adult models who read and were interested in reading were important, and that an abundance of books and magazines was generally available to those children. Reading to a child as early as the age of one gives him a statistically significant head start.

As cited earlier, the influence of Head Start and compensatory programs and the appeal of American Montessori schools to the affluent are indicants for parental support. A cursory examination of popular magazines and the claims of those who sell educational materials for home consumption often include an emphasis related to early reading instruction. It is not uncommon to find children entering school who already have developed reading skills. As Durkin documents, such an advantage persists in those children.

Mason (*17*) surveyed a racially, socioeconomic, and intellectually stratified sample of preschoolers and found that 94 percent of them would *like* to learn to read. Motivation is there, both parental and for the child.

Research

Research to date has not been definitive; much of it has been too fragmented to be of real value even though, as noted by Samuel Weintraub, "In the past three years alone, well over 1,100 published reports and summaries of research have been identified and abstracted in the annual summary of reading research. Of the topics covered by these reports, more research was reported on beginning reading than in any other area. How children learn to read has been a topic of high interest to reading researchers since the very beginnings of published research. The intense research focus on this aspect of reading may be due in part to the importance and drama attached to learning to read."

A comprehensive approach, such as the Targeted Research and Development proposed by the United States Office of Education as a longitudinal project, is serving as a reading research guide for the 1970s. This project, and others similarly comprehensive, could focus upon a convergence technique for reading research. Such a convergence technique as blending elements from system-program analysis, philosophy of education, learning theory, and group dynamics could provide a comprehensive approach and test every aspect of a selected model. The project—if successful—could provide:

- research of existing approaches and concepts of reading instruction
- theoretical researching of reading itself
- exploration and the manipulation of instructional sequences

- refinement of materials
- adjustment of other instructional variables.

From such a prototype, an instructional reading system, usable within public school classrooms, may emerge. Within the decade, this approach may answer many of the basic questions about reading.

The prime responsibility for reading programs, however, will remain at the local level and will be dependent upon local programs and resources. Teachers are often inundated by the sheer amount of information, and a critical analysis and compilation of the truly significant and more important research data would help if research findings are to receive broader application. In this day, when research papers, periodicals, books, and similar materials are produced more rapidly than any one person can read, what is needed is an information dissemination system—a means of closing the gap between what the researchers know and providing the information to teachers but in a usable, understandable form.

A review of the many articles, research, and publications pertaining to early reading instruction which have been reported over the past decade reveals a general theme that becomes readily apparent. The bits and parts fit together comprising a generalized pattern. This pattern posits the need to match early childhood educational procedures with each child's optimal rate of intellectual development and a satisfying life (*9*).

Readiness

Readiness is more than the result of maturation or the combination of the abilities most reading readiness tests seek to assess. As typically conceived, readiness is a two-edged sword which commits many to failure while at the same time insults the capabilities of others. Rather, reading readiness should be viewed as a synergistic result of maturation, facilitated by instruction and enhanced through training of visual discrimination abilities. In this connection, it has been pointed out that letters, words, and three-dimensional objects are superior to geometrical abstractions and two-dimensional objects in the assessment of readiness. The question of readiness is being viewed as a *propaedeutic* function; namely, that when a child learns to read, he does so a step at a time—the vital requirement being that he is *ready* to learn the first step which, in turn, prepares him to be ready for the second step. We need to view reading readiness as a set of abilities which makes one child ready for one kind of instruction while another child may be better matched with another kind of instruction (*6*).

Matching Reading Instruction and Readiness

The objective then becomes to generate adaptive, useful behavior among children during their life spans when they are most susceptible to change. This task will require that reading instruction during these early years take into account the developmental level of each child as an individual to attain the proper "match" of which Hunt (*10*) speaks. If there is success built in for the child and if the climate of a positive self-fulfilling hypothesis is advanced, the positive impact of instruction will likely be enhanced.

Structured Reading and "Childhood"

Some claim that childhood is being truncated; that our modern, urbanized, congested society does not permit children to be children; and that the imposition of a structured program, such as reading instruction, will impinge upon the teacher's being able to provide a warm, motherly love. Fowler, Moore, and others have countered that children often respond to structured reading instruction with no apparent loss of childhood experiences. In fact, the case can be made that, by being able to interact better with the symbols of their environment, the age-span of childhood is enhanced. Weintraub states, "In all the areas looked at, research has scarcely scratched the surface of what can and must be done. For the researcher, the challenge is there; for the practitioner, it promises new insights, better answers, and worthwhile applications."

Conclusions

Our task in the 1970s is to consolidate what is known about early childhood education and about reading. We must conclude the soap opera antics and embark upon a revitalized format based on the "how" and "what" of reading. Let us acknowledge the demise of the "when factor" and relinquish the security of research reruns which add very little to the understanding of reading instruction. Let us also embark upon an implementation and dissemination campaign. Our purpose is clear; our blueprint for success is emerging. To paraphrase a television commercial, we've come a long way, baby, to get where we are today; but, we still have a long way to go.

References

1. Bloom, Benjamin S. *Stability and Change in Human Characteristics.* New York: John Wiley and Sons, 1964, 88.
2. Bloom, B. S., et al. *Compensatory Education for Cultural Deprivation.* New York: Holt, Rinehart, and Winston, 1965.
3. Cicarelli, V. G., et al. "The Impact of Head Start: A Reply to the Report Analysis," *Harvard Education Review,* 40 (1970), 105-129.
4. Cohen, S. Alan. *Teach Them All to Read.* New York: Random House, 1969, 127.
5. Deutsch, Cynthia P., and Martin Deutsch. "Brief Reflections on the Theory of Early Childhood Enrichment Programs," in R. D. Hess and R. M. Bear (Eds.), *Early Education.* Chicago: Aldin Publishing Company, 83-90.
6. Dunn, Barbara J. "The Effectiveness of Teaching Selected Reading Skills to Children Two Through Four Years of Age by Television," unpublished doctoral dissertation, University of California at Los Angeles, 1969.
7. Durkin, Dolores. *Children Who Read Early.* New York: Teachers College Press, Columbia University, 1966, 133-139.
8. "Early Childhood Education Issue," IDEA *Reporter,* Winter 1969, 2.
9. Fowler, W. "The Effects of Early Stimulation," in R. D. Hess and R. M. Bear (Eds.), *Early Education.* Chicago: Aldin Publishing Company, 1968, 28-29.
10. Hunt, J. McVicker. *Intelligence and Experience.* New York: Ronald Press, 1961, 362-363.
11. Karnes, Merle B., et al. "An Evaluation of Two Preschool Programs for Disadvantaged Children: A Traditional and a Highly Structured Experimental Preschool," *Exceptional Children,* 34 (1968), 667-676.
12. Kelley, Marjorie, and M. K. Chen. "An Experimental Study of Formal Reading Instruction at the Kindergarten Level," *Journal of Educational Research,* 60 (1967), 224-229.
13. LaConte, Christine. "Reading in the Kindergarten, Fact or Fantasy?" *Elementary English,* 47 (March 1970), 382-387.
14. Langston, Genevieve. "Achievement of Gifted Kindergarten and Gifted First Grade Readers," *Illinois School Research,* 3 (1966), 18-24.
15. McKee, Paul, and Joseph E. Brzeinski. *The Effectiveness of Teaching Reading in Kindergarten,* Cooperative Research Project No. 5-0371. Denver: Denver Public Schools, 1966.

16. McManus, Anastasia. "The Denver Prereading Project Conducted by WENH-TV," *Reading Teacher,* 18 (1964), 22.

17. Mason, G. E. "Preschoolers' Concepts of Reading," *Reading Teacher,* 21 (1967), 130-132.

18. Morrison, Coleman, and Albert J. Harris. "Effect of Kindergarten on the Reading of Disadvantaged Children," City University of New York, ERIC, ED035512, 1968.

19. Robinson, Helen. "Significant Unsolved Problems in Reading," *Education Digest,* February 1971, 42-45.

20. Schoephoerster, Hugh. "The Final Report to the Maud and Louis Hill Family Foundation on Teaching Skills Basic to Reading," unpublished paper, Anoka-Hennepin School District, Anoka, Minnesota, 1969.

21. Sutton, Marjorie H. "Children Who Learned to Read in Kindergarten: A Longitudinal Study," *Reading Teacher,* 22 (1969), 595-602.

22. Weintraub, Samuel. "Reading Research for the Schoolman: A Look at Some Aspects of Learning to Read," *Phi Delta Kappan,* April 1971, 490-493.

23. Zaruba, Elizabeth A. "A Survey of Teachers' Attitudes Toward Reading Experiences in Kindergarten," *Journal of Educational Research,* 60 (1967).

HOW MAY BEGINNING READING STRATEGIES BE "BEST" INTEGRATED AND ARTICULATED WITH THE TOTAL LANGUAGE ARTS PROGRAM?

Margaret Early
Syracuse University

presents some specific strategies.

COMPONENTS OF A LANGUAGE ARTS PROGRAM IN THE PRIMARY GRADES

Children enter primary grades at the height of their learning power. They have proved their prowess by mastering the sound system of their language by the age of three, and they are well on their way to mastering the grammatical system, a process they will complete by the age of eight (*1*). They have learned to make language work for them through speaking, questioning, demanding services, voicing their likes and dislikes, labeling and classifying things around them, identifying their world, listening, enjoying the sounds of language, getting answers to their questions, and finding out about themselves and others. They have learned many of the rules that govern language; they don't confuse nouns with verbs, they know how to form plurals and tenses. Any errors they make are the result of applying rules consistently (e.g., *foots* and *catched*) to words that are exceptions to the basic principles.

Children have gained all this remarkable power over language informally—not without help, but without consciously structured help. The more opportunities they have had to interact with adults and older children, the richer is their vocabulary and the more fluent their sentences.

Ruth Strickland pointed out that teachers can learn three things about children if they listen to their talk. First, the quality of a child's language reflects the language of his home and neighborhood. Second, the vocabulary a child uses tells something about the breadth of his experiences, real and vicarious, and the extent to which he has talked them over with adults and older children. The quality of his language—whether it is standard or nonstandard—reveals nothing about his IQ; "he learned what there was to learn and learned it as best he could with his own power." Third, how he uses language tells much about his self-concept; whether he is confident and outgoing or timid and repressed (*2*).

The fact that children have learned to talk, not through imitating adults, but through figuring out the rules of language, is perhaps the most impressive sign we have of their learning power. But there are others. The intellectual curiosity of five-to-six-year-olds is at a high pitch; they want to know something about everything (but not everything about something). For normal children, the attention span expands and contracts, as it does for adults, according to interests and tastes. The same children who fidget and yawn as they wait their turn in the reading group can sit wide-eyed and motionless through a Saturday morning of cartoons and commercials.

If children enter primary grades with a formidable record of successful learning behind them and with momentum to continue to learn, the crucial question for teachers is how to insure that they leave the primary grades with that momentum preserved, and, if channeled, not extinguished. Educators have been so unsuccessful in answering that question that today many people are talking about "alternatives to school" and proposing that education burst through the restrictive walls of an institution. Here and there across the country there are experiments in "schools without walls"; storefront schools; and liberated versions of the old colonial dame schools. We find some knocking down of the walls within public schools as we move toward open classrooms. And we have dreams of melding a highly technological computerized instruction with the kind of free-flowing spirit of Plato's Academe. Such dreams, we are told, are, even now, a technological possibility; what prevents their being an immediate reality is that we are psychologically unready for them.

Meanwhile, for most children, the school with walls is today's reality, and, once they enter those walls, the free and individualized learning they know outside must be diminished. This is inevitable, for public schools are meant to serve large numbers, and any massing of individuals imposes restraints. Thus, it is only natural for a teacher put in charge of twenty-five children of a similar age but very dissimilar levels of maturity to look for ways to group them for instruction. Unfortunately, that search has often resulted in some unnecessary restraints being imposed for the comfort of the teacher and to the discomfort of would-be learners.

Nevertheless, granting that the school has overdone it, the need for structure and order is obvious. It could be argued that schools are serving society when children learn as members of groups, as well as individually. But surely the transition from a free to a restricted learning environment ought to be made as easy as possible. Indeed, that was the purpose of the children's garden—the kindergarten—to help children to get ready for the more structured environment of the next grades. There was a time during the 60s when it appeared that the kindergarten might lose its essential informal character and become a downward extension of first grade; another room where children were grouped for teaching them to read. That trend is being modified, fortunately, and kindergarten is once again becoming the first open classroom, where some children, as they are ready, can notice written language and begin to make discoveries about the rules that govern the writing system.

In helping children make the transition from self-initiated, unguided learning to the more directed learning of the classroom, kindergartens seem to be on the right track. If, in spite of kindergartens and preschools, the transition is still too abrupt, the fault is in the too rigid structuring of the primary grades. Hence the move in the last decade or so to break out of the eggcrate structure of the traditional elementary school; hence the move toward nongrading, team teaching, and individually prescribed instruction; hence the appearance of new school buildings with "learning pods," tutoring booths, carrels for independent study, centrally located media libraries, teacher planning centers, cluster classrooms with retractable walls, mobile storage units, and other architectural innovations. School planners and architects are, of course, way ahead of taxpayers and teachers. They are also ahead of teacher training institutions, research and development teams, publishers, and film producers. So it is not surprising in schools that are architecturally open to find teachers building walls from bookcases and screens, staking a claim in which to conduct the usual kinds of lessons. Or in independent study centers to find children copying pages from an encyclopedia. Nor should we be surprised when team teaching experiments rigidify into a sorry kind of departmentalizing. Such problems are a natural consequence when teachers try to adopt innovations without fully understanding *why*.

It is too bad that teachers have to run to catch up with technology and new school design. No doubt it would be better if teaching ideas shaped the environment, rather than the other way around. Still, we should be grateful that possibilities for innovation are waiting for us.

How do we get ready to take advantage of them? First, by knocking down the psychological walls that divide the curriculum into watertight compartments even in the primary grades. Thus, it is appropriate to consider the components of a language arts curriculum rather than a reading program. Reading and writing are extensions of the total process of language acquisition begun in infancy and, viewed as such, provide a philosophical base for reconsideration of how teachers can assist in the process. We take a further step when we consider how reading and writing, as well as talking and listening, serve children in learning in every other aspect of the curriculum.

Two items have high priority on the kindergarten teacher's list of things to do: one is to provide outlets for children's creative energies; the second is to find out how far each child has come in his language development.

Everything in a good kindergarten room is directed toward these ends: the familiar corners for playing house and store; the collections of living and growing things—plants, flowers, fish, turtles, gerbils; the bins of strange and common objects that excite children's senses and stimulate their imaginations; the art corner where ideas can be expressed in paint and clay and other media; the workbenches where children can literally hammer out ideas; the outdoor play areas where children can stretch their imaginations as well as their muscles. Dancing, miming, dressing up, making believe, listening to stories read by the teacher or recorded by others, looking at books, walking tours of school and neighborhood, visits to airports, firehouses, children's museums—all these feed the imagination and loosen tongues. And the wise teacher listens!

The kindergarten is a large and busy place for very good reasons, but there must also be periods of quiet. However, when the teacher turns off talk, she must have a legitimate purpose. Listening to a story or to music, or watching a film, filmstrip, puppet show, or a performance by other children are good reasons. Waiting one's turn to respond to a workbook exercise or matching letter shapes on a ditto sheet have low priority—when they enter the kindergarten curriculum, they come *after* the needs for thinking, feeling, expressing, and talking have been satisfied.

In an integrated language arts program, writing begins early. As soon as children can use fingerpaints, hold a brush, crayon, or pencil, they can create a picture. Soon they can tell a teacher or older friend a story to go with the picture, perhaps at first just a title or a caption. In kindergarten they may "write" in this sense both individual stories and group experience charts. By the time they enter first grade they are very familiar with print and the reasons for writing. They have seen teachers write directions, poems, stories, weather, news, and lists of room helpers on the chalkboard. In kindergarten, or at home in front of the television set, they have learned to recognize many letters, match letters, find them in words, and name some letters. In first grade they begin tracing and writing letters in manuscript, and this practice reinforces their learning of letter names and sounds. Soon they are tracing and writing words which they will encounter in their preprimers.

Having mentioned preprimers, let's consider the place of basal readers in the total language arts program. They are there, and usually in a central position, because most teachers want the security of a well-organized program based on the systematic introduction of new words and the consistent repetition of the words introduced. Because basal series provide this security, they should liberate the teacher rather than restrict her. With a consistent line of reading development as the core of a total language arts program, the teacher is free to modify, enrich, and elaborate upon basic plans, confident that she will not overlook essential skills. While the teacher can borrow a measure of confidence from a well-organized system for teaching reading, she has also to bring self-confidence to the task, enough so that she uses a series critically, selectively. The basal series can become a deadly weapon in the hands of the timid teacher who fears to omit anything and who follows the manual without any understanding of its purposes—or her own. This is the teacher who understands very little about children, or how they learn to read. If the majority of them learn to read, and they usually do, it is because they have figured out the system in spite of the teacher.

Wise decisions as to what to omit from a basal program depend on the teacher's skill in analyzing children's progress in reading. Diagnostic teaching is the skill, or art, that is what we really mean when we say that the teacher, not the method, makes the difference. Knowing what to leave out of a basal program and knowing what to include in an individualized program is a matter of knowing how, whether, and in what ways each child is learning.

Using a Basal Reader Program Selectively

Teachers tend to stick closely to the directed reading lesson and to use all the skills exercises, workbook pages, and ditto sheets that the publisher can provide. They tend to leave out the "related activities," the follow-up enrichment which develops language arts and skills other than reading. This is unfortunate, especially so if the time is squandered on drilling children who either "have" the particular skill or are not yet ready for it. No responsible teacher wants to minimize decoding, whether her approach is basal oriented or wholly individualized, but how much emphasis is the optimum can be determined only with reference to real children. Not every child needs every exercise in a packaged program; some children need more practice or a different kind.

The same kind of balance needs to be maintained in the development of comprehension, the main focus of the directed reading lesson. Not every child nor every group, needs all the purpose setting questions posed by the manual, nor all the dissecting of meaning that follows every selection.

The skillful teacher is as wary of asking too much as too little. With fast moving and average groups, she frequently assigns a whole selection to be read silently without interruption and checks on comprehension through open discussion, not too prolonged. With slower moving groups, it is just as important to place the lesson to their abilities and interests. If the teacher finds herself asking this group too many questions and badgering the children to get answers, the material is probably beyond their instructional level. When skills development is carefully coordinated with the text to be read, and specific skills preparation precedes the reading, then children can be trusted to read the selection.

What about the suggestions for enrichment? These suggestions frequently are glossed over, but should *not* be. Of course the teacher selects according to her total plan. At the beginning of each new book, the teacher should study all the suggestions for enrichment and gather for the library corner as many as possible of the listed books, filmstrips, and recordings. Some of these will be used quite independently, others she may want to reserve for a special tie in with a basal lesson. If the teacher skimps the manual's suggestions for enrichment because she has better ideas herself, that's quite all right; if she skimps to save time for phonics or filling in blanks in the language workbook, she is undermining the language arts program. For the teacher with few ideas of her own, the enrichment sections of basal manuals offer a core around which a total language arts program may be developed quite easily, with strong relationships to what the children are reading. Teachers will find excellent suggestions for personal writing, as well as writing stimulated by reading or listening to stories; for studying word meanings and their functions in sentences; for relating art and music to reading; for developing library skills; for creative dramatics and improvisation. These are all components of a total language arts program.

Nearly all primary teachers incorporate into a basal program certain components of what has become known as "individualized reading."

Children select their own books and pursue personal reading at their own pace, sometimes concurrent with group instruction in a basal; sometimes for a six-to-eight week interval between, or after, basal readers. Teachers try to include individual conferences, easing themselves and their children out of exclusively group instruction. Nevertheless, finding time remains the biggest problem. Some teachers substitute conferences for group instruction with the fast readers while retaining the slower readers in group instruction. Others find that individualizing other aspects of the curriculum, such as mathematics, spelling, and word skills, making use of programed materials and learning activities packages, releases them for more conferences. Even teachers who have abandoned grouping entirely, frequently worry about time for individual conferences.

As an answer to these worries, proponents of individualized reading are forced into proposing schedules and formulas for "conferencing" which may distort the real purposes. The immediate solution seems to be to increase the ratio between pupils and adults, bringing in volunteers, paraprofessionals, and high school and college student aides.

A more basic solution may come from asking why conferences are necessary anyway. To lend moral support? To evince interest? To show we care? To stimulate more reading? To diagnose learning? To teach word skills? To clarify matters of comprehension? To open up a child's thinking? All of these are good reasons, but some are better than others. Some require professional teaching competence, others can be achieved by any sympathetic adult or older child. Some require a quick check; others a thoughtful, relaxed conversation. Some could be achieved just as well, or better, in groups.

The answer to how much time for conferences depends on two factors: the abilities of children to learn on their own, and the degree to which teachers resort to individualized reading as a single approach. The more securely children learn the basic skills in the beginning, the more freedom they should be permitted in pursuing their own interests. The individual conference is an apron string operation, not at all characteristic of freedom to learn.

We need to look not only for better ways to individualize on a one-to-one basis, but how to individualize within the group. Can we get rid of waiting one's turn in the group? Can we have children answer in unison, either by holding up cards or fingers, or, on occasion, orally? Can we replace reading around the group with partnership reading?

Individualized learning has quite limited values in the total language arts program. It is no good at all for developing speaking and listening. Reading and writing, though they are solitary pursuits, both profit from discussion before and after.

As we reinforce connections among the language arts and break down walls within the whole primary curriculum, we would do well to improve our techniques for working with groups, as well as with individuals. Every teacher needs to experiment with groups of different sizes and composition.

In a grade three classroom, the day begins with everyone working on his own, some reading, others finishing up a science project from the day before, some taking a spelling test that has been taped, some children writing in their journals or day books. After thirty minutes or so, the teacher calls together a first group for reading instruction and subsequently this group breaks into pairs for partnership reading. For the next twenty minutes, the teacher checks with children who are pursuing information for a social studies report. As she forms another reading group, other children begin to work in twos, threes, or fours.

Several times during the day she calls the whole class together, once to introduce a new unit in science, another time to talk over a class project for parents' night, later to listen to the next chapter in a book she is reading to them.

In the beginning of the year, this grade three teacher was constantly on call, flitting from one child to another, from group to group, sorting out materials, settling differences, answering questions, helping Susan find the right word for her poem or Fred to find the right reference on butterflies. As the year progressed she found she could confer longer with individuals and groups as the children learned to do more for themselves. Now and then she had a chance to observe and record her notes on individuals, although most of this log keeping still had to be done at the end of the day.

The more fluid and flexible the language arts program is on the surface the more firm it must be at its foundations. Essential to the structure is the teacher's ability to diagnose language skills. What kinds of questions does a child have ready answers for? Do his errors in oral reading show that he is not paying attention to context? Does he consistently confuse certain vowel digraphs? Does he skip strange words or miss syllables when he tries to identify long words? Does this child read voraciously and spell creatively? Does one spell and punctuate meticulously but have trouble drawing inferences and recognizing main ideas?

What reasons lie behind the performance? The question, basically, is what kind of child is this who reads and writes in these ways?

Almost anyone can administer informal—or formal—reading tests, but skill in interpreting test results is the mark of a professional. Once an accurate interpretation has been made, knowing what to do about it is still further proof of professionalism. More and more, the professional teacher's role may be to diagnose and prescribe, while aides take over the actual routines of helping children to follow the prescriptions. This will be especially true in the development of language skills; in the development of the arts of language—just as in the related arts of mime, music, sculpture, and painting—the role of the teacher has become one of friendly critic, consultant, and fellow practitioner.

It should be clear by now that the major components of the language arts program are children and teacher—and books. Trade books, matched to the range of children's reading abilities; works of contemporary and classic literature for the teacher to read aloud; picture books to be pored over by the youngest, read, admired, and imitated by the older children; all kinds of reference texts and fact-finding books for children; lots of nonfiction trade books and textbooks, including basal series.

I'm less sure about language arts textbooks in the primary grades. But books about language, yes. There are a dozen or more of these, from alphabet books to *The First Book of Codes* and *Ciphers and All About Language,* from which young children can learn as much as they presently need to know about the nature and history of language. And lots of poetry books from which the teacher and children can select poems to read aloud.

Most important of all to a total language arts program are the books children write themselves, their journals and day books if they want to share them, and the books they write for their library table. In a first grade room in October, the children shared their own books with me. For one collection the teacher had printed just two words, "I like __________" and each child had drawn a picture of what he liked and dictated the end of the sentence, after which the teacher bound them together in a book for all to share. Others in this collection included "My pet likes __________," "I wish I had __________," "My mother (or father) is __________."

In a third grade, by Christmas, the children had a whole collection of books they had written, illustrated, and bound themselves. Many of these concerned what they were discovering about numbers and shapes;

they were works of nonfiction, complete with tables of contents and indexes. Books of haiku, cinquains, and other verse forms are commonplace these days.

Books written by children to be read by their peers illustrate one way of integrating the language arts. More important, the publication of children's writing (on the ditto machine, that is) gives significance to communication. Some writing is for oneself alone (and, as such, serves therapeutic purposes, helping children to think and feel and express), but most writing is to say something to someone else. Publication makes real the need for precision and clarity, as well, perhaps, as heightened expression. Moreover, children should select what is to be published, as they should decide what is to be put on the bulletin board and what is to be discarded. Thus, they begin to develop criteria of excellence and improve their insight and taste, as well as their writing.

Although reading and writing have been emphasized, it is necessary that we are aware that we live in an increasingly oral culture, and contemporary language arts programs reflect that fact. One reflection is seen in the tremendous upsurge of interest in creative dramatics in the last several years. Where it was once considered something of a frill, it is now recognized as central to the education of the imagination, to the heightening of sensitivity. Teachers at every grade level are flocking to workshops to learn how to free themselves for improvisation and how to encourage this kind of involvement in others. They are using improvisation in all areas of the curriculum.

In a reading lesson, for example, role-playing is a means of quickening children's interest in a story to be read, or of deepening their understanding of a problem to be encountered. After reading, role-playing is often the natural way to extend concepts and reinforce comprehension. Similarly, role-playing, since it imbues children with a sense of history, is a cornerstone in social studies inquiry and discovery.

A language arts program that is sealed off from the rest of the curriculum has little validity. Even in the primary grades, children apply the skills of language in learning content, and teachers must be ready to help them make these applications. If a group is using a social studies or science textbook, the teacher guides them in the same way as in a directed reading lesson. Indeed, one could argue that the directed reading lesson is more appropriately applied to content reading than to stories that do not need to be remembered. This is one reason why today we are finding much more nonfiction even in beginning reading materials. With the growth of independent study, we realize that study skills must begin early. Readiness for reading for main ideas begins in first grade as children learn to classify. They learn to follow a time sequence, not just in narratives, but in descriptions of a process such as paper making. And they read to follow directions for making a toy automobile, a bound book, or a papier-mâché puppet. By their third year of reading development, children are learning to identify a topic, to seek out and select pertinent information, to take notes, and to evaluate critically what they read and what they hear.

In these comments on a total language arts program there is a conspicuous lack of attention to usage and grammar. So far as usage is concerned, the omission implies that skills such as punctuation, plurals and possessives, forming tenses, and achieving sentence variety are best taught incidentally in connection with reading and writing. Any good basal series calls attention to the way writers punctuate and why they use paragraphs. Every good teacher helps children to use the conventions of written language as they need them.

The omission of grammar is deliberate. I see no reason for formal study of syntax or parts of speech in primary grades.

There is, of course, the very serious question of what to do about children's nonstandard dialects. In the beginning, teachers should use the language children bring to school. That means using the children's grammar in experience charts at first, retaining however, standard spelling. Gradually, the teacher introduces standard plurals, possessives, and verb tenses in dictated stories and, as soon as possible, introduces children to the standard dialect in preprimers and picture books. Of course, she speaks and writes her own version of the standard dialect, but she can role-play in other dialects. The important point is that she *accepts* the child's home dialect and admires his proficiency in it.

Conclusions

We began by considering the awesome feats of learning that children manage before they enter school, and we wondered how we could preserve and cultivate their will to learn throughout the primary grades. We urged that many elements of the informal kindergarten be extended to the years beyond, so that a proper balance is struck between learning on one's own and learning in groups. We suggested that removal of psychological barriers within the curriculum should precede—certainly accompany—the knocking down of physical walls within the school.

References

1. Smith, Frank. *Understanding Reading.* New York: Holt, Rinehart and Winston, 1971.

2. Strickland, Ruth. "Children before Methods," *Report on Reading Conference.* New York: New York University, 1968.

ARE THERE SOME "BEST" STRATEGIES FOR TEACHING PHONICS, DECODING, BLENDING, AND OTHER WORD ANALYSIS SKILLS TO BEGINNING READERS?

Duane R. Tovey
Wisconsin State University

provides some answers on phonics.

RELATIONSHIP OF MATCHED FIRST GRADE PHONICS INSTRUCTION TO OVERALL READING ACHIEVEMENT AND THE DESIRE TO READ

The purpose of this study was twofold: to determine the degree to which phonics instruction at the eighth month of first grade is matched to the specific abilities of individual children identified by Botel's *Phonics Mastery Test* (*1*), and to determine the relationship of matched phonics instruction to overall reading achievement and the desire to read.

Related subproblems:

1. How many children are receiving *matched** phonics instruction after having demonstrated on the Botel Test that they are ready for phonics instruction on *one* of the following levels?
   a. *above* first grade level (short, long, and other vowel sounds)
   b. *later* first grade level (consonant blends and digraphs)
   c. *early* first grade level (initial consonants)
   d. *prephonics* level (undeveloped auditory and/or visual discrimination skills and other abilities necessary for success in phonics)
2. Do significant differences exist in children's *overall reading achievements* between matched and mismatched groups?
3. Do significant differences exist in children's *desires to read* between matched and mismatched groups?

* Children were identified as receiving matched phonics instruction when instruction was found to be in accordance with their specific phonics abilities as identified by the Botel Test; i.e., instruction was confined to the phonics level to which a student was assigned.

Procedures

Procedures used:

1. Twenty first grade classrooms (526 children) were randomly sampled from the 173 first grade classrooms in the selected school district (midwest industrial community of approximately three hundred fifty thousand). Stratified random sampling procedures were employed to ensure a sample representative of all academic types of schools (high, average, and low).*
2. Botel's Phonics Mastery Test was administered to determine the phonics abilities of the first grade children in the sample.
3. The degree of match between specific children's phonics abilities and their instruction was determined by a) placing components of phonics instruction on a developmental continuum, b) plotting individual *achievement* (by level) on the given continuum, c) plotting individual instruction (by level) on the given continuum, and d) analyzing and recording the relationships between individual phonics achievement and instruction as indicated in b) and c) according to the academic rating of schools.
4. The relationship of matched and mismatched phonics instruction to overall reading achievement was ascertained by a) determining overall reading scores on the *California Reading Test* (*3*) and b) employing *t* tests to determine the significance of difference between the means of children with matched and mismatched phonics instruction.
5. The relationship of matched and mismatched phonics instruction to children's desires to read was ascertained by a) utilizing opinions of teachers in the sample concerning the degree to which their children like to read a lot, a little, or not at all and b) determining the relationship of children's desires to read to the match-mismatch dichotomy by inspection.

Findings

Table 1 shows that of the 526 pupils in the study, 44 (8 percent) were found to be receiving matched instruction. The high academic

* Schools were classified as high ($\geq$ 83rd percentile), average or low ($\leq$ 18th percentile) academic schools, based on composite scores of the *Iowa Tests of Basic Skills* (*2*).

TABLE 1
NUMBER OF CHILDREN RECEIVING 1) MATCHED AND 2) MISMATCHED PHONICS INSTRUCTION

Type of School	Matched Instruction	Mismatched Instruction	Total
High Academic	—	136	136
Average Academic	21	194	215
Low Academic	23	152	175
Total	44	482	526

schools had *no* matches. Twenty-one (10 percent) of the children in average academic schools received matched instruction while twenty-three (13 percent) in low academic schools received matched instruction.

The teaching patterns for children found ready for instruction at each of these levels follow.

Data Concerning Children at the Above First Grade Level

Table 3 shows that of the 39 children who were ready for *above first grade instruction, none* were found to be receiving instruction matched to their abilities, i.e., long, short, and other vowel sounds.

Note that most of the 39 children (N = 26) were from high academic schools. Note also that the difference between the number of children found ready for *above first grade* instruction in average and low academic schools was negligible.

TABLE 2
NUMBER OF CHILDREN FOUND READY FOR PHONICS INSTRUCTION AT GIVEN LEVELS

Type of School	Above First Grade Level	Later First Grade Level	Early First Grade Level	Pre-Phonics Level	Total
High Academic	26	62	44	4	136
Average Academic	7	60	94	54	215
Low Academic	6	56	64	49	175
Total	39	178	202	107	526

TABLE 3
INSTRUCTION RECEIVED BY CHILDREN FOUND READY FOR ABOVE FIRST GRADE PHONICS (N = 39)

Type of School	Matched Instruction	First Grade Instruction	Both On and Above First Grade Instruction	Total
High Academic	—	5	21	26
Average Academic	—	3	4	7
Low Academic	—	6	—	6
Total	—	14	25	39

Most of these children in the *above first grade category* (N = 25) were found to be receiving instruction which was both on and above first grade level.

Data Concerning Children at the Later First Grade Level

Table 4 indicates that 178 children were found ready for *later first grade* phonics instruction (consonant blends and digraphs). Of these, 36 were found to be receiving matched instruction.

None of the children in high academic schools, who were found to be ready for *later first grade* instruction, was found to be receiving matched instruction. The difference between the number of children with matched instruction in average and low academic schools was negligible. Most of these children (N = 142) were found to be receiving mismatched instruction. The diverse instruction received by these 142 children is analyzed in Table 5.

TABLE 4
INSTRUCTION RECEIVED BY CHILDREN FOUND READY FOR LATER FIRST GRADE PHONICS (N = 178)

Type of School	Matched Instruction	Mismatched Instruction	Total
High Academic	—	62	62
Average Academic	19	41	60
Low Academic	17	39	56
Total	36	142	178

TABLE 5

MISMATCHED INSTRUCTION RECEIVED BY CHILDREN FOUND READY FOR LATER FIRST GRADE PHONICS (N = 142)

Type of School	Above First Grade	Above and Later First Grade	Above, Later, and Early First Grade	Above and Early First Grade	Later and Early First Grade	Early First Grade	Total
High Academic	—	—	29	—	33	—	62
Average Academic	—	10	18	10	3	—	41
Low Academic	1	—	7	27	—	4	39
Total	1	10	54	37	36	4	142

Note that the largest number of these children (N = 54) was found to be receiving instruction at all levels.

Data Concerning Children at the Early First Grade Level

Table 6 shows that 202 children were found to be ready for *early first grade* instruction (initial consonants). Of these, seven were found to be receiving matched instruction. The remaining 195 pupils were found to be receiving mismatched instruction.

TABLE 6
INSTRUCTION RECEIVED BY CHILDREN FOUND READY FOR EARLY FIRST GRADE PHONICS (N = 202)

Type of School	Matched Instruction	Mismatched Instruction	Total
High Academic	—	44	44
Average Academic	2	92	94
Low Academic	5	59	64
Total	7	195	202

A greater percentage of matches was found in low academic schools than in average academic schools, with *no* matches in high academic schools. The mismatched instruction received by most of these children (N = 195) is analyzed in Table 7.

Most of these children were found to be receiving phonics instruction either on the *later and early* first grade level (N = 77) or on the *above, later, and early* first grade level (N = 53).

*Data Concerning Children at the Prephonics Level**

Table 8 shows that 107 children were ready for prephonics instruction only. Of these pupils *one* child was found to be receiving instruction matched to his abilities. Fifty-one were found to be receiving first grade instruction even though they were not ready for such experiences. Fifty-five were receiving a combination of first grade and above first grade level instruction, which was mismatched to an even greater degree.

Note that only four of the prephonics children were from high academic schools. Even though more pupils (N = 54) were found in average academic schools than in low academic schools (N = 49), a greater *percentage* of these pupils was found to be in low academic schools (more children were sampled in average schools). Notice fur-

* Pupils who identified *less than three* initial consonants correctly on the Botel Test.

TABLE 7

MISMATCHED INSTRUCTION RECEIVED BY CHILDREN FOUND READY FOR EARLY FIRST GRADE PHONICS (N = 195)

Type of School	Above First Grade	Above and Later First Grade	Above, Later, and Early First Grade	Above and Early First Grade	Later and Early First Grade	Later First Grade	At the Pre-phonics	Total
High Academic	—	—	15	—	29	—	—	44
Average Academic	—	5	35	22	10	20	—	92
Low Academic	4	—	3	—	38	13	1	59
Total	4	5	53	22	77	33	1	195

TABLE 8
INSTRUCTION RECEIVED BY CHILDREN FOUND READY FOR PREPHONICS INSTRUCTION ONLY (N = 107)

Type of School	Matched Instruction	First Grade Instruction	Both On and Above First Grade Instruction	Total
High Academic	—	2	2	4
Average Academic	—	17	37	54
Low Academic	1	32	16	49
Total	1	51	55	107

ther that most prephonics students (N = 55) were found to be receiving instruction both on and above first grade level.

Data Relating Overall Reading Achievement to Matched Phonics Instruction

A significant difference was found to exist ($t = 3.58$, $p < .05$) between mean scores of matched and mismatched groups on the *California Reading Test* (3) for children in average academic schools. Such a significant difference, however, was not found in low academic schools. No tests of significance were calculated for high academic schools due to a lack of any matched instruction.

This section of the study was extended to determine the relationship between matched phonics instruction and overall reading achievement for boys and girls from both average and low academic schools.

A significant difference was found to exist ($t = 3.33$, $p < .05$) between mean scores for boys in average academic schools (N = 127); however, such a significant difference was not found for boys in low academic schools (N = 95).

No significant differences were found to exist between mean scores for girls in either average (N = 88) or low academic schools (N = 80).

Data Relating the Desire to Read to Matched Phonics Instruction

Significant differences were observed in children's desires to read between matched and mismatched groups for boys in both average and low academic schools; that is, boys in average and low academic schools with matched phonics instruction desire to read more than those with mismatched instruction. These differences were determined by inspection.

Conclusions

The evidence gathered from the findings of this study suggests that:

1. Most of the phonics instruction in the given school district is *not* matched to the specific abilities of children.
2. Children in high academic schools are receiving instruction in phonics that is too easy for them while children in average and low academic schools are receiving instruction in phonics that is too difficult.
3. Children who are ready for *above first grade level* phonics instruction are receiving instruction that is too easy.
4. Most children who are ready for *later first grade level* phonics instruction are receiving instruction that is sometimes too easy and at other times too difficult.
5. Children who are at the *early first grade level* and at the *prephonics* level are receiving instruction that is too difficult.
6. The phonics instructional patterns employed by teachers in the given school district are many and diverse with little relationship to children's abilities.
7. The matching of phonics instruction to children's specific abilities has a limited relationship to overall reading achievement and the desire to read.
8. The matching of phonics instruction to the abilities of children in average academic schools is of more consequence than in low academic schools.
9. The matching of phonics instruction to the abilities of boys is of more consequence than to that of girls in both average and low academic schools.

References

1. Botel, Morton. *Phonics Mastery Test.* Chicago: Follett.
2. Lindquist, E. F., and A. N. Hieronymus. *Iowa Tests of Basic Skills,* Form 1. New York: Houghton Mifflin, 1955.
3. Tiegs, Ernest W., and Willis W. Clark. *California Reading Test,* Lower Primary, Form W. Monterey, California: California Test Bureau, 1957.

GERALD G. GLASS
Adelphi University

provides some answers on decoding which result from experience in two separate federally funded programs: a summer remedial program at Brentwood, Long Island, and an all-year program in the New York City schools.

DECODING ONLY?

The learning-to-read process is, first, learning to decode and, then, learning to "read." This rationale assumes, for instructional purposes, that decoding or identifying the sound of the word is only associatively related to reading, reading being defined as minimally including understanding the printed word. If one thus orders the reading process, it becomes apparent that the ability to identify a sound is different in substance and dimension from the ability to respond to the word in either isolation or specific context. Learning to decode is based more upon repetitions of sound-symbol correspondences than upon the many-dimensional intellectual learnings that are the substance of reading.

Method

The teachers in the projects worked with small groups and with individuals. The primary material used was approximately 1,000 word cards included in the five decoding kits published by Easier-To-Learn materials. The cards are arranged in 125 word-groupings according to the common letter clusters. (Those clusters were identified by the author in an examination of the words introduced in two major basal series.) In each training session two or more "cluster" groupings were classified and studied according to the visual and auditory structure of the whole word.

In the training sessions the learner never sees less than a whole word. Whole words are seen in context only when students do oral reading at sight from a basal reader for practice purposes. Students are conditioned by selective questions that elicit responses focusing on visual and auditory associations made with common letter clusters in whole words. Twenty words or less are utilized with each letter cluster in either the initial, medial, or final position.

The goal is to have the learner eventually respond habitually to the word structure that contributes most to the sound of the whole word. As was mentioned in the introduction, the ten- to fifteen-minute lessons include only the teaching of decoding and are concerned with reading, that is, meaning. Children in the program are told that they will be able to read *after* they learn to decode.

Populations

A total population of 217 (112 boys and 105 girls) was divided into three first grades, two second grades, two third grades, two fourth grades, one fifth grade. The program ran in P.S. 20 Queens three times a week for 30 weeks. The second program was in the Brentwood summer school. Daily instruction for a total of 42 instructional days was given to 42 boys and 14 girls. Although most of the students were in third, fourth, and fifth grades, a few were in the sixth grade. All students in the Brentwood program were identified as remedial readers. Students were chosen by the teachers for extra work in the summer decoding clinic because of significant below-grade reading levels.

Scoring

Test results are reported in terms of the pretest and post-test scores on the word analysis section of the Durrell Analysis of Reading Difficulty. The norms are expressed in grade levels. A classification of low (L), middle (M), and high (H) is given for each grade level based upon the number of words identified correctly, but the results reported here are expressed in ordinal numbers.

Durrell's classification of L, M, and H at each grade level does not lend itself to expressing mean measures of change in decoding ability. To be able to report change in a valid and reasonable manner, five points were assigned to change from one classification (L, M, H) to another. If the pretest score was at a low third grade level and the post-test score was at a middle third grade level, the change would be a one-classification change and, thus, a five-point change (approximately four to five months growth). If the change in score went from low second grade level to low third grade level, the change would be 15 points, i.e., from low second to middle second to high second to low third (more than one year's growth).

Results

P.S. 20 Queens. Average improvement for the 217 youngsters was approximately two years (24 points). There was no significant difference in the improvement of the boys versus the girls. For the three first grades (containing many non-English speaking children) the improvement approximated one year and a half (15.7 points). There was no significant difference between the boys versus the girls. Both second grades improved more than two years (28.6 points). The girls' improvement was approximately one-half year greater than the boys'. Both third grades improved slightly more than two years (27.6 points). There was no significant difference between the improvement of the boys versus that of the girls. Both fourth grades improved slightly more than two years (27.1 points). There was no significant difference between the boys and the girls. The single fifth grade improved two years (25 points) with no difference between the boys and the girls.

Brentwood Summer School. The overall average gain for the 56 students was slightly less than one year (10.4 points). The boys' average gain was approximately four months less than the girls'. (However, because of the small *n,* the chi-square was not significant.) The students were tested on the 220 Dolch Sight Words before and after the program. There was an overall improvement of 35 percent. (Unfortunately, no statistical significance can be placed on the 35 percent improvement because a percentage score requires another score to test significance.)

Discussion

The P.S. 20 Queens study ran for the full school year. The average improvement of two years included the many "disadvantaged" first grade youngsters who did not progress further than letter identification. (Only one child did not learn to identify all the letters in the alphabet at sight.) This segment of the first grade population offset a large group of first graders who made dramatic strides in their learning to read.

Although the school is not primarily composed of disadvantaged minority youngsters, more than 30 percent of the students in the instructional program were from the minority disadvantaged group. The normal prediction for the school had been somewhat less than one year's growth as a result of one year's instruction. It is apparent, then, that the average growth reported is significant, not only as one looks at the whole school but increasingly so as one sees the improvement made by individual youngsters predicted to make less-than-normal growth.

As an indication of the program's acceptance, the ten teachers involved in the program for the 1969-1970 year volunteered to be in the 1970-1971 program. In addition, requests came from more than half of the teachers in the school to include the perceptual conditioning program in their reading curricula.

The Brentwood summer remedial program improvement of just less than one year in the seven weeks that the program was run was highly significant. The change becomes dramatic when we consider the expectancy level of the children who attended the summer reading center. They were all children who in the past had not made normal developmental growth in reading. They had been identified as remedial and in need of extraordinary help beyond the classroom situation. Nearly 80 percent of the youngsters were either Blacks or of Puerto Rican descent.

A reasonable prediction for the summer reading group assumed that these students would make less than average improvement (if any at all) in any remedial reading program. Considering the juxtaposition of the facts that the group averaged only 33 instructional sessions and improved approximately one year of reading ability in spite of low growth expectancy makes one take heart with the results.

Approximately 28 teachers worked in both the developmental and the remedial projects. Except for the first grade classes in the Queens project, all classes and groups in both projects reported improvement statistically similar to average improvement for each program. This is a strong indication that a great majority of teachers were able to produce uniformly effective results. It is probable, then, that in these programs the perceptual conditioning strategy significantly affected the reported improvement.

MIRIAM BALMUTH
Hunter College

reports some answers from a study of blending skills and raises some additional questions to be answered.

PHONEME BLENDING AND SILENT READING ACHIEVEMENT

The study here described was undertaken to develop an instrument to measure phoneme blending of nonsense syllables and to investigate the relationship of this skill to silent reading achievement. The questions of whether blending can be taught, how it is related to intelligence, its relation to auditory abilities, whether it is a unitary function or may derive from more than one source, and, importantly, its relation to reading achievement have never been fully answered.

A survey of the literature pertinent to the present study indicates that phoneme blending has not been clearly defined, understood, or measured. Confusion is revealed by the variety of synonyms that have been applied to this ability (auditory blending, auditory synthesis, smoothing, sound blending, vocal phonics), all of which overlook the specifically linguistic nature of the units to be blended.

The process of blending, in almost every case, requires the ability to change the given allophone of a phoneme into another allophone of the same phoneme according to its position in the completed syllable. Thus, the /t/ that is pronounced when the word "cat" is presented in its unblended form (c-a-t) is very different from the /t/ that is pronounced when the word is correctly synthesized (cat). What actually occurs, then, is the combining of *phonemes* rather than of "sounds" or "auditory" units, which is why the term *phoneme blending* is used here.

A second source of confusion about phoneme blending refers to its physiological origins. It has often been assumed that it is a function of the peripheral nervous system, much in the manner of auditory acuity and auditory discrimination; and a number of investigations have included phoneme blending as one of several auditory factors.

For some time, however, there has been evidence to indicate that blending ability is a function of the central nervous system and is highly specific. In 1970, Geschwind reported several cases of adults who, due to brain injury, had lost the ability to read written words but were able to read numbers. In such a case, the written word "six" would not be recognized while the written number "6" would be, since it is a logogram rather than alphabetic and does not require the blending of phonemes. Similarly, Zerbin-Rudin reports the case of a Japanese boy with reading difficulty in the "Kana" (alphabetic Japanese writing system) who had minimal difficulty in the "Kanji" (logogramic writing system). Although both Geschwind and Zerbin-Rudin reported after the present study had been completed, their data are neat confirmations of the discrete and nonauditory nature of phoneme blending.

Phoneme Blending and Reading Achievement

When studies of the relationship between phoneme blending and reading were examined, it was found that although there had been awareness of this factor among investigators in the field of reading as early as 1790, relatively few controlled studies are available. While these tend to indicate a positive relation between the two factors, there is some disagreement and questions have been raised about the validity of the findings because of the tests used to measure blending.

Hypotheses

For the present study, as a start toward the clarification of phoneme blending, three hypotheses were formulated and tested. The first hypothesis stated that there would be a positive relationship between the ability of elementary school boys' phoneme blending of nonsense syllables and their silent reading achievement. In the second hypothesis, the same relationship was theorized for elementary school girls. Third, it was hypothesized that the relationship between the two variables would be similar for both boys and girls.

Procedure

An original test was devised to measure phoneme blending of nonsense syllables since only tests measuring phoneme blending of meaningful words were in existence at the time of the study. Phoneme blending of nonsense syllables rather than of words was used to circumvent the possibility of children's guessing at a whole word on the basis of several recognized sounds. In addition, the ability to blend sounds in unknown word syllables rather than in recognized or known words is an integral part of the skill of syllabication. Therefore, a nonsense syllable blending test might help to identify children who are not progressing beyond early reading levels because of their being hampered by blending difficulties not revealed by word blending tests.

Added features of the test included the presence of a wide range of phonemes in various positions within syllables. Items that contained phonemes that were prone to auditory discrimination confusion (th and TH are examples) were eliminated.

The odd-even technique was used to establish reliability for the test, and a coefficient of .88 was obtained. An item analysis was made for each item of the test and resulted in item discrimination and item difficulty indices. These indicated that the test items discriminated very well between high and low scores and that the test was rather difficult for the sample population. This relative difficulty is an advantage, since the resultant high ceiling makes it suitable for older children.

The final form of the experimental test was then administered to 252 boys and girls, randomly selected from grades one to six with 21 boys and 21 girls from each grade. Care was taken to select a sample typical of the wide ethnic and socioeconomic range of the total New York City school population.

Additionally, although no hypotheses had been formulated concerning them, the variables of age, sex, and ethnic origin were examined in relation to phoneme blending of nonsense syllables.

Results

Results of the study support the basic hypotheses. A highly significant positive relationship (.66) between phoneme blending and silent reading achievement was found for the 105 boys in grades two through six. Similarly, a highly significant positive relationship (.56) between phoneme blending and silent reading achievement was found for the 105 girls in grades two through six. The difference between these two relationships was not significant.

Highly significant relationships between phoneme blending and age and between phoneme blending and ethnic origin were found for the sample of 252 children in grades one through six. The relationship between phoneme blending and sex was not significant.

Conclusions

Conclusions reached on the basis of the results of the study include:

Phoneme blending of nonsense syllables can be reliably and validly measured.

There is a positive relationship between phoneme blending of nonsense syllables and silent reading achievement among elementary school children.

The sex of a child does not affect the relationship between phoneme blending and silent reading achievement.

The sex of a child does not affect the child's phoneme blending ability.

Older children, on the whole, are better blenders of nonsense syllables than are younger children although there are children at every age who have difficulty with this ability. First grade children, especially, find phoneme blending of nonsense syllables difficult.

New York City children of European ethnic origin are better blenders on nonsense syllables than are New York City Black children or children of Latin American ethnic origin. The fact that the children in the study were New York City children is emphasized here because these differences in blending ability may very well be related to language and socioeconomic factors which are more related to the implications inherent in the geographical location of a specific ethnic group than to the ethnic group itself.

Implications

The extent to which phoneme blending can be taught and the extent to which it results from normal maturational processes have not been settled. However, in view of the high correlation between phoneme blending and reading, and as long as there is a good chance that this ability can respond to teaching, it behooves both classroom teachers and remedial reading teachers to determine the phoneme blending ability of their students and, wherever necessary, to incorporate phoneme blending instruction in their reading programs.

In view of the relationship between phoneme blending and age, teachers of the primary grades should be especially alert to blending instruction. However, since there were children of every age who had blending difficulty, teachers of the intermediate grades should also be alerted to the importance of blending ability and should determine the blending abilities of children who are having reading difficulty. Instruction can then be given in those cases where blending difficulty is present in order to help those children who can profit from such instruction.

In as much as there is a significant relationship between blending and ethnic origin and between blending and reading achievement, teachers of children whose ethnic origins have been demonstrated to have lesser blending ability should make extra efforts to incorporate blending instruction into their reading programs.

A final implication of the present study is that it contradicts the widely held opinion that girls are more proficient in language abilities than are boys. In the present study, both phoneme blending ability and the relationship between phoneme blending and silent reading achievement were not significantly different for boys and for girls. In fact, there was a nonsignificant trend in favor of the boys regarding phoneme blending ability itself. Furthermore, the silent reading achievement of girls was slightly higher than that of the boys, but the difference was not significant. The implication of these findings is that girls, as a group, may have no greater advantage in language skills than do boys.

Suggestions for Further Study

A major goal of this study and in developing this test was the stimulation of further investigation of phoneme blending. The study generated the following suggestions for research:

1. The relationship of blending and intelligence should be examined.
2. Auditory memory and blending should be examined further. Many children who were not able to blend a test item were able to state it in unblended form.
3. An investigation of phoneme blending by mentally retarded, hard-of-hearing, and brain-injured children, as well as by children with articulatory defects, would help to refine our understanding of the roles of intelligence, auditory acuity, brain injury, and articulation in blending.
4. A study of the relationship of phoneme blending to oral reading would be useful, since children who have blending difficulty may be able to derive meaning from context on silent reading tests and, thus, not reveal the extent of their need for better blending skill.
5. Studies might be made of the relationship of phoneme blending of nonsense syllables to phoneme blending of words, perhaps using

a word-blending test constructed on the criteria used in developing the present test.

Finally, since it is clear that some phonemes and combinations of phonemes are more difficult to blend than others, it would be fruitful to investigate the relative difficulty of blending various combinations of phonemes. This knowledge would be most helpful at arriving at certain sequences of blending instruction which teachers of reading might utilize

References

1. Balmuth, Miriam. "The Relationship between Phoneme Blending of Nonsense Syllables and Silent Reading Achievement Among Elementary School Children," unpublished doctoral dissertation, New York University, 1966.

2. Geschwind, Norman. "Anatomical Mechanisms of Acquired Disorders of Reading," invited address, 78th Annual Convention of the American Psychological Association, Miami Beach, Florida, 1970.

3. Zerbin-Rudin, Edith. "Kongenitale Wortblindheit Oder Spezifische Dyslexie (Congenital Word Blindness)," translated from the German by Steven G. Vandenberg, *Bulletin of the Orton Society,* 17 (1967), 47-54.

ARE LINGUISTICS STRATEGIES "BETTER" THAN TRADITIONAL PHONICS IN TEACHING BEGINNING READING?

DORIS V. GUNDERSON
United States Office of Education

finds values in using some linguistics strategies.

ARE LINGUISTIC PROGRAMS DIFFERENT?

Some publishers have produced basal reading series which they term linguistic. Is a linguistic program simply a classroom program in which the medium of instruction is the "linguistic reader"? Many linguists do not consider those readers linguistically based.

Rystrom (*7*) defines a linguistic reader as "any set of reading materials in which the phoneme-grapheme correspondences presented in the text have been sequenced." In his summary of the second grade phase of one of the first grade reading studies comparing various methods of teaching reading, Dykstra (*5*) says that the various materials included in the linguistic approach possessed most, if not all, of the following characteristics:

1. There is an early introduction to letters, and knowledge of letter names and the ability to recognize letters are considered prerequisite skills for reading instruction.
2. Sound-symbol relationships are taught through careful sequencing of word patterns. Words with high sound-symbol regularity are taught first, and the child is led to discover the sound-symbol relationships which exist. In many cases, the child is encouraged to use sound-symbol relationships as the basic word recognition technique by withholding from him such clues as pictures and word length.
3. In many cases, there is less emphasis on understanding and comprehension in the early stages. Reading is considered a process of translating graphic symbols into sounds, and primary attention is paid to helping the child learn the decoding system.

Dietrich (*4*) observes that in some linguistic readers, in addition to teaching the phoneme-grapheme relationship, attention also is given to syntax, pitch, and stress and that a few of the newer series are beginning to stress comprehension. Seymour (*9*) insists that a linguistic approach to reading instruction points out the priority of speech and that it demonstrates that writing is merely a way of recording that same speech by the use of symbols. Consequently, a child who is taught reading by a linguistic approach should understand that if he can speak, he can also learn to read and to write. He knows that he will be in control of the symbols he uses to represent his language; the symbols will not control him. Sabaroff (*8*) echoes those views by saying that a linguistic approach helps children break the code and understand the operational system.

According to Barney (*1*), the professional literature is literally glutted with "so-called research studies" which attempt either to prove or to disprove the relative merits of the analytic, synthetic, or whole-word methods of teaching. He reasons that a teacher should know how to use all three methods effectively but that a knowledge of historical linguistics will help to determine which word should be introduced with which method. He goes on to say that historical linguistics can be a tool for teachers in eliminating the use of abbreviations by rote, applying silent letter combinations through sheer memory only, or other practices he considers questionable.

The rationale and logic of historical linguistics underlying the uses and changes of languages make it easier for the teacher to determine the relative importance of what, why, how, and how much of an item should be taught. Jones (*6*) values the importance of the teacher's knowledge of linguistics in teaching reading by saying that the teacher should understand thoroughly the linguistic structure of the language she is using as a medium of teaching.

These may be inadequate definitions of a linguistic reader, but can the use of a linguistic reader in the classroom be equated with a linguistic program? Certainly a linguistic program should include more activities than those offered in a basal reader, be it linguistic, phonic, or whole word. A linguistic program should recognize the relationship between the various aspects of language and reading processes and should take advantage of the accumulated knowledge of research in language acquisition and reading.

Research studies concerned with language and reading may contribute more to the teaching of reading than the comparative and/or contrastive methodological studies. Some studies have been directed to the way in which reading should be taught to children who speak a dialect different from the language of the school. One theory is that children should learn to read in their own dialect, e.g., Black English reading materials for children who speak Black English. Another theory is that dialect-speaking children can learn to read Standard English and that dialect interference will not affect the process of learning to read.

Rystrom's study, conducted in rural Georgia and replicating an earlier study in California, was designed to determine if Black dialect is a cause of reading disability. Three hypotheses were investigated:

1. Black children can be taught to use features of White speech which do not occur in their native dialects.
2. Knowledge of this additional dimension of dialect will have a positive and significant influence on word-reading scores.
3. The use of phoneme-grapheme-controlled readers will have a positive and significant influence on word-reading scores.

The population consisted of four first grade classes in an all-Black school in Georgia. Rystrom examined the effects of dialect training upon children learning to read from two different types of reading series: a traditional basal reader and a linguistic basal reader. The control group used a traditional basal reader and received no dialect training. Two experimental groups were given dialect training, with one using a traditional series and the other a linguistic series. The third experimental group also used a linguistic series but was given no dialect training.

During the first semester all four groups concentrated upon the readiness skills presented in the basal series. At the beginning of the second semester, two experimental groups switched to the linguistic readers and two groups received 20 minutes of language treatment daily for 80 days.

Two instruments were used as pre- and post-test measures. The Rystrom Dialect Test was used to evaluate dialect change attributable to dialect training, and the Gates Word Reading Test was used to indicate improvement in word reading. The reading sections of the Stanford Achievement Test were administered as post-tests to provide an index of general reading ability. The statistical technique employed was analysis of covariance with the pretest scores used as the covariate.

The results reject all three hypotheses. Analysis of the data does not indicate significant differences between groups on dialect performance. The dialect test scores of the groups who did not receive dialect training are essentially the same as the performance scores of the groups who had training. No production differences occur. The data from the Gates test does not indicate increased recognition of phoneme-grapheme controlled correspondences as a result of the dialect training, and the use of phoneme-grapheme controlled readers does not have a significant influence on word reading scores.

Rystrom concludes that a dialect-training program does not significantly increase the reading achievement scores of children who speak a Black dialect; dialect training, in fact, has a negative effect upon their decoding skills.

Williams and others (*11*) conducted a study to determine whether a positive relationship exists between grade-level reading achievement and oral-language performance. The population included 60 children from five schools, with 20 each from first, third, and fifth grades, all from low socioeconomic backgrounds. The subjects were chosen by the classroom teachers on the basis of two factors: subjects were considered to have average academic ability and to be nonfailures in the classroom. The IQ range on the California Test of Mental Maturity was from 95 to 110. The teachers indicated that the subjects were reading in an average group.

The grade level of each pupil's oral language was estimated by showing him three pictures from the Chandler Language Arts Series during the seventh month of the school year. Each pupil was asked three series of three questions with each series designed to initiate sequentially a literal, an interpretive, and a critical level of thought responses. The children's oral reactions were tape recorded and transcribed to provide an objective evaluation. Using the Botel Readability Formula, the average grade level of each pupil's oral language was determined from the recorded responses obtained from the three series of questions.

Results of the study indicate that the girls made no gains in level of oral conversation during the first five years of school and that the boys gained only between first and third grades. The investigators conclude that for girls the present teaching methods are of no consequence in developing oral language achievement, and for boys the methods appear to increase their oral expression solely during the beginning school years. The data suggest that the present methods may be helpful only to those of very low language skills, particularly boys during the first school years.

Although Williams and his coinvestigators acknowledge that the study was exploratory with a small, not entirely random sample of pupils of average mental ability from a low socioeconomic level, they suggest that the present teaching of oral vocabulary is inadequate and that there is a necessity for recognizing appropriate and effective oral language teaching procedures. The investigators feel that their findings concur with other recent research which associates both inadequate oral language development and limited reading progress with three contributing causal factors: low economic home environment, middle grade peer slang influence, and poor teaching techniques.

Prediction may serve a useful purpose in diagnosis. If at the beginning of first grade or even earlier a child's probable success or failure in reading could be estimated, the teacher could focus instruction on those particular aspects of reading with which the child is likely to encounter difficulty. Since language and reading are so closely related, it seems reasonable to assume that oral language might be a predictor of reading success.

Bougere (*2*) investigated the predictive role of oral language competency for success in beginning reading. Her study was based on the rationale that the components of linguistic maturity presumed to be related to reading success have not been clearly identified. From her synthesis of findings of investigations of children's oral language development, she hypothesized that promising indices of oral language development included mean length of communication unit, ratio of sentence-combining transformations to communication units, ratio of subordinate clause length to length of communication unit, and measurer of extent and diversity of vocabulary.

The study attempted to answer three questions:

1. Do selected factors identified in previous research as indices of maturity in children's use of oral language show a significant relationship to first grade reading achievement?
2. Do any selected oral language factors or combinations of these factors predict level of reading achievement as accurately as does a standardized reading readiness test?
3. How much do specific oral language factors and combinations of these factors add to the predictive value of a standardized reading readiness test?

The population consisted of 60 pupils in a south Chicago suburb who were attending first grade for the first time: two schools were located in a predominantly upper-middle-class neighborhood, two in a middle class, and two in a lower class.

Two types of reading achievement predictors were examined and compared: the Metropolitan Readiness Test and seven experimental measures of syntactic and vocabulary factors in oral language selected on the basis of an extensive review of the previous research literature. Other measures included the Kuhlman-Anderson Test, the Gray Oral Reading Test, and three subtests of the Stanford Achievement Test. Bougere conducted individual interviews to obtain the language measures; the tapes were transcribed and analyzed syntactically.

Analysis of the data led Bougere to draw several conclusions. The value of the Metropolitan Readiness Test as a predictor of first grade word recognition achievement can be significantly increased by the addition of a measure of oral vocabulary range plus a measure of oral vocabulary diversity. An even greater increase can be produced by the addition of all the experimental linguistic predictors used in the study. The value of the Metropolitan as a predictor of first grade comprehension achievement can be significantly increased by the addition of a measure of average *T*-unit length. However, the value of the test as a predictor of first grade achievement in vocabulary or in oral reading cannot be significantly increased by the addition of any one or any of several combinations of the linguistic predictors used in this study.

Bougere lists several practical implications which are helpful to first grade teachers who wish to assess the linguistic competency of their pupils. The child's volubility in the classroom is a highly doubtful indicator of his linguistic competency as it is related to reading achievement. The most useful predictors are mean *T*-unit length and range and diversity of vocabulary. Results of the study indicate the need for repeated and varied oral language observations. The teacher who desires a dependable assessment of the pupil's linguistic competency must extend his observations beyond the classroom to children in varied situations.

After reviewing numerous studies in oral language acquisition, Brittain (*3*) reports that when children enter school they generally have not mastered English morphology. She hypothesized that some of the difficulties children experience in learning to read may be due to a pedagogical failure to recognize and adapt to their level of oral linguistic development.

The objectives of her study were to assess the relationship between children's inflectional performance and reading achievement and to explore possible grade and sex differences in these relationships. Brittain first assessed children's learning of inflectional rules and then examined the relationship between reading achievement and inflectional performance.

The measure of inflectional performance used was a revision of Berko's test; subjects were 79 first and 55 second grade children in a suburban northern Virginia community. Results of the individually administered test support the hypothesis that in the child's oral linguistic development the application of inflections proceeds from the simple to the complex. Performance on the simple items was similar for both first and second grade children, but the second graders performed slightly better on the complex items. No differences between sexes in inflectional performance were found. Apparently the traditional linguistic superiority of girls does not hold true for the area of morphological ability measured by the test.

The number of subjects used in analyzing the relationship between reading achievement and inflectional performance totaled 56 first and 52 second grade children. The Primary Reading Profiles and the Lorge-Thorndike Intelligence Test were used to measure reading achievement and intelligence. Brittain found a significant relationship between inflectional performance and reading achievement at both first and second grade levels and suggested several explanations. Two sorts of information are provided by inflections: 1) semantic information signaling number, tense; and 2) grammatical information marking words as members of form classes, such as nouns and verbs. Which of these two aspects is more important for reading comprehension is not clear; both may be relevant. Inflectional skill may contribute to reading ability by providing congruence between incoming visual stimuli and speech responses to which they may be attached.

As anticipated, the correlations between reading ability and inflectional performance increased from grade one to grade two. Brittain attributed this increase to two factors: 1) the marked increase in the number of inflected forms in basal reading materials from first to second grade and 2) the possibility that some children who have completed second grade still have not mastered the morphophonological rules of their language and evidence a genuine linguistic retardation which could hamper their progress in reading.

Why girls show greater facility than boys in the process of becoming literate was answered only partially and in a negative fashion in the study, but apparently the superior early reading achievement of girls is not due to superior inflectional skill.

Brittain concludes that morphology has structural significance in the process of learning to read and considers her findings both linguistically and psychologically relevant for beginning reading.

If this relatively minor component of the English grammatical system contributes significantly to the reading achievement of first and second grade children, then certainly the development of children's linguistic abilities should be prerequisite to the initiation of formal instruction in reading.

Materials used in teaching reading have long been under attack; frequently the criticism is concerned with the subject matter: It may be alien to the children reading it, it may be dull, or there are too many or too few illustrations. Claims are made that the vocabulary in basal reading series is controlled. The language patterns, however, are less often related to the language children use in speaking.

Tatham (*10*) investigated the relationship between reading comprehension and materials written with select oral language patterns at second and fourth grades. The relation of sex differences to reading comprehension of the patterns was also considered, for the investigator hoped to contribute to the dialogue of those who have found significant sex differences in language abilities.

Three questions were posed:

1. Do significantly more second and fourth graders comprehend material written with frequent oral language patterns better than material written with infrequent oral language patterns?
2. Do fourth graders comprehend material written with frequent and infrequent oral language patterns significantly better than second graders?
3. Do second and fourth grade girls comprehend material written with frequent and infrequent oral language patterns significantly better than second and fourth grade boys?

Two reading comprehension tests were constructed for the study: Test A included language patterns that appear frequently in the oral language of both second and fourth grade children, and Test B was comprised of language patterns that appear infrequently in their oral language. The tests were a series of sentences with three pictures drawn for each sentence. The reader selected the picture that best described the sentence and drew a line from the sentence to the picture. The paragraph meaning section of the Stanford Achievement Test was also administered.

The population consisted of 7 second and 6 fourth grade classrooms in two elementary schools in Madison, Wisconsin. The mean IQ on the Lorge-Thorndike was 105.6 with a range from 76 to 145. All of the subjects were from a middle socioeconomic background.

Analysis of the data reveals that a significant number of subjects attained a higher reading comprehension score on Test *A* (which included language patterns that appear frequently in oral language) than on Test *B*. Fourth graders scored higher on both tests than second graders; an anticipated finding since reading is a skill which improves with practice and experience. Girls did consistently better than boys, but the difference was not significant.

Tatham lists several implications of her study. It is both logical and consistent with linguistic knowledge to use children's patterns of language structure in written material to facilitate learning the concept that spoken and written language are related. The findings suggest that children would benefit from control over sentence patterns until they can untangle word relationships in any number of infrequent patterns. Writers of children's materials should consider the use of language patterns that are easiest for children to comprehend when the goal is maximum comprehension. Tatham feels that vocabulary control is not the only logical nor most desirable control when comprehension of language structure is essential.

Conclusions

The studies reviewed here do not tell a teacher how to teach reading; rather, they provide information which can be applied in reading instruction. They indicate that 1) a linguistic program involves more than the use of a linguistic reader; 2) the activities carried on in classrooms should be based on the accumulated knowledge from research in *both* oral language and reading; 3) the teacher's knowledge about oral language and linguistics is vital to the understanding of readiness for reading.

It is obvious that of the presently available reading programs those which publishers call "linguistic" do not, in fact, supply all the needs that are desirable in a linguistic program. In general, the programs do provide for structured teaching of letters and sound-symbol relationships. Some do show concern for the fact that writing is a written form of oral language. Some even indicate that oral language is a matter of stress and intonation as well as words and letters. Basically linguistic reading programs are designed to teach "code-breaking," confined primarily to breaking a spelling code.

A desirable linguistic program should contain much more than a teachable analysis of the spelling code of written language. It is quite obvious that written language is related to and based upon oral language.

Yet the Williams study indicates that oral language ability does not improve under present school teaching practices except for underachieving boys and then only in the first years of school.

That dialect differences may affect oral language learning and particularly learning to read has been hotly debated. Yet Rystrom's study indicates that teaching designed to aid children with dialect differences does not achieve the desired result. Bougere's study demonstrates the importance of the relationship of oral language vocabulary and the child's use of sentences to his achievement in reading comprehension. Brittain's study indicates that children's skill in the morphological aspects of language is significantly related to reading success. The final point of inquiry of the examined studies was that of the content of linguistic reading programs. Here the Tatham study shows clearly that materials written in the natural language patterns of speech are more successfully read than materials written in the typical reader patterns. The hypothesis that oral language patterns are more important to control than vocabulary is obvious.

At this point it appears that a linguistic program has yet to be written which will meet criterion and objectives as follows: 1) provide the teacher with definite means of determining the oral language readiness of the children to be instructed, 2) provide the teacher with means of building upon the oral language of the children to be instructed, 3) provide for teacher instruction in those aspects of linguistics important to a complete understanding and demonstration of oral and written language, 4) provide for materials of diagnosis and instruction for continued development of oral language competence, and 5) provide reading content developed according to natural oral language patterns.

Existing linguistic programs are different from either the phonics readers of the past and present or the "look-and-say" readers of the immediate past in that they focus upon a more reasonable attempt at breaking the spelling code. They are not truly "linguistic," however, for they do not provide the kind of diagnosis or instruction that will help children who speak dialects other than Standard English to attain the language and reading competence of which they are capable. In fact, it is highly probable that the oral language development of an average or superior child is not aided and may even be harmed by existing reading programs.

References

1. Barney, Le Roy. "Linguistics Applied to the Elementary Classroom," *Reading Teacher,* December 1970, 221-226.
2. Bougere, Marguerite. "Selected Factors in Oral Language Related to First Grade Reading Achievement," *Reading Research Quarterly,* Fall 1969, 31-58.
3. Brittain, Mary M. "Inflectional Performance and Early Reading Achievement," *Reading Research Quarterly,* Fall 1970, 34-48.
4. Dietrich, Dorothy M. "New Approaches to Easing Word Attack at the Beginning Reader Levels," *Reading Teacher,* March 1970, 511-515.
5. Dykstra, Robert. "Summary of the Second Grade Phase of the Cooperative Research Program in Primary Reading Instruction," *Reading Research Quarterly,* Fall 1968, 49-74.
6. Jones, Daisy M. "The Implications of Linguistics for the Teaching of Reading," *Elementary English,* February 1969, 176-183.
7. Rystrom, Richard. "Dialect Training and Reading: A Further Look," *Reading Research Quarterly,* Summer 1970, 581-599.
8. Sabaroff, Rose E. "Improving Achievement in Beginning Reading: A Linguistic Approach," *Reading Teacher,* March 1970, 523-527.
9. Seymour, Dorothy Z. "The Difference Between Linguistics and Phonics," *Reading Teacher,* November 1969, 99-102.
10. Tatham, Susan Masland. "Reading Comprehension of Materials Written with Select Oral Language Patterns: A Study at Grades Two and Four," *Reading Research Quarterly,* Spring 1970, 402-426.
11. Williams, Maurice, Edith Weinstein, and Ralph O. Blackwood. "An Analysis of Oral Language Compared with Reading Achievement," *Elementary English,* March 1970, 394-396.

JOHN R. ROGERS
Texas Technical University

rejects the concept that there is one *linguistics method and suggests an end to the controversy.*

LINGUISTIC PROGRAMS—ARE THEY REALLY DIFFERENT?

Part of the confusion—if not outright bewilderment—that has prevented linguistics from making contributions to reading instruction in consonance with its undeniably great potential arises from the syntactical truth that *linguistics* is a singular noun; it, therefore, properly takes a singular verb. We say, "linguistics is," not "linguistics are." It is understandable, then, that great numbers of people who have not had direct training in linguistic science have assumed it to be a unitary branch of learning—comparable, for instance, to chemistry or psychology. As it is syntactically correct to speak of *the* science of linguistics, it would appear reasonable to expect its contribution to reading instruction to be made under a more-or-less unitary system that might be spoken of as *the* linguistic method of teaching reading.

The difficulty arises from the fact that, although the word *linguistics* is syntactically singular, it is logically and pragmatically plural. Logically, we should not say "linguistics is," but "linguistics are." Linguistics is not a simple, unitary branch of learning. Rather, it is made up of a remarkably diverse—and diversified—collection of fields of study that are loosely related through common concern with the scientific study of language.

Here, however, their unitary relationships end. Each of the various and independent branches which go to make up this loosely defined science of linguistics has its own central points of focus, its own special methodologies, and its own special ground and house rules for carrying on workaday affairs.

Orthography, morphology, lexicography, syntax, dialectology, linguistic geography, etymology, and semantics are but a representative few of the many disciplinary mansions which make up the collective house of linguistics. Each of these and other branches of linguistic science proceed relatively independently of every other branch.

Obviously, then, *the* linguistic method of teaching reading must await that probably remote day when some linguistic Copernicus will discover the key which will unify the various fields of linguistics into a truly monolithic whole. Until that day arrives, we reading specialists will do well to organize our attempts to apply linguistic knowledge to reading in accord with facts as they are.

For the time being, at least, we must reject *the* linguistic method of teaching reading as nothing more than a rather ill-conceived academic shibboleth. By the same token, we must reject, also, all programs which have the temerity to represent themselves as being *the* linguistic method of teaching reading or as being based on *the* linguistic method.

There go, then, most of the currently available "linguistic" programs of reading instruction. And there stands, also, by implication at least, the answer to the question, "Linguistic programs, are they really different?"

To some degree, of course, every reading program is influenced by knowledge from several fields of linguistics. Beyond that basic input common to all, so-called linguistic programs of reading instruction are likely to be uniquely different to the degree that they have been deliberately shaped by specialized input from one or more branches of linguistic science. Unquestionably, some linguistic reading programs really *are* different from what may be described as a typical reading program. "Different," however, is not necessarily synonymous with "better."

The Contributions of Linguistic Science

Phonology (*phono,* sound; *logos,* study), that broad branch of linguistics which deals with the sound structure of language, numbers among its sub-branches two and—if you are willing to be broadminded about it—three which are of particular interest to the reading teacher. *Phonetics* focuses primarily on the production of speech sounds, and *phonemics* focuses on the function of speech sounds. A difference between two speech sounds is phonetic if it can be discerned, and phonemic if it makes a difference in meaning. The difference between /pæt/ and /pæt⁻/ is phonetic. The difference between /pæt/ and /pæd/ is phonemic.

For the reading teacher, phonemics and the light which it can shed on the forty-odd phonemes or individual speech sounds of English have a great deal to offer. SRA's DISTAR program is an example of a formal attempt to harness the tremendous linguistic horsepower of phonemics directly to reading's wagon.

Every reading teacher should take a course in phonemics, not for the purpose of acquiring content which she will teach directly to children but rather to gain solid foundation material for her own understanding of a related member of the linguistic family.

Phonics is an additional factor in linguistics. Orthodox linguists would, for the most part, take a dim view of phonics' bid for membership in the family. Quite properly, they would insist that linguistics encompasses only those branches devoted to the *scientific* study of language. And it is not to be denied that phonics is hardly scientifically based. Instead of following the prescribed laws of discovery and organization which generate the content of other branches of linguistic inquiry, phonics can only be described as loosely associated collections of rules which have been iterated and preserved over the years by practicing elementary school teachers. If there is one thing about which they would agree, it is that there is disagreement concerning the "true" set of phonics rules which lead to reading Mecca. In short, phonics can aptly be described as the "folk medicine" of linguistics.

However, there are few today who would relegate phonics to the educational limbo to which it was assigned between World Wars I and II. We may not agree about the proper content of phonics, but we *are* agreed that reading is largely a decoding process and that decoding requires the use of phonics.

The task of the phonemicist is a relatively simple one. He has only to learn the 40 phonemes of English, learn to describe and recognize them, learn the proper symbol or grapheme to represent each speech sound—and he's in business. His task is that of going from the spoken sound to a graphic representation of it.

The task of the teacher who attempts to help a child go from the grapheme to the phoneme which it represents is vastly more difficult. Because our conventional alphabet of 26 letters must represent 40 phonemes, the orthographer or spelling specialist must resort to various ruses to stretch the 26 symbols to cover their assigned task of encoding.

The reading teacher must appeal here to the at-best-only, near-scientific field of phonics. Fortunately, serious students are working to move phonics into full scientific membership in the academic community.

The literature offers extensive guidance concerning the long-enduring question of just which phonics generalizations should be taught. There appears to be no proper comprehensive answer to the question. It is possible that it must be answered separately for each child. The typical child, however, can probably profit from a direct knowledge of:

1. The letters of the alphabet—name, form, and serial order.
2. The short sounds of the vowels, together with the notion that closed syllables usually contain short vowels.
3. The sounds usually represented by single consonant letters and consonant digraphs.
4. Soft *c* and *g* and their usual orthographic diacritics.
5. The long sounds of the vowels. The final *e* diacritic is probably worth knowing if it is clearly understood that it doesn't work every time. In the cases of single vowel letters, a sensible procedure is to try the short sound first; if that doesn't make sense, try the long sound. So far as vowel digraphs are concerned, awareness is probably enough.
6. The diphthongs and their usual spelling patterns.
7. The fact that post-vocalic *r* usually causes the preceding vowel to have a sound which is neither its long nor short sound—so easy a generalization that most youngsters pick it up unaided.

Most readers have grapheme-phoneme relationship knowledge far beyond those recommended. If much *formal* attention is required beyond this point, however, the case probably borders on the clinical.

Orthography (*ortho,* right; *graph,* write), the science of writing (actually spelling) words correctly, has a great deal to offer the reading teacher. Spelling is worth teaching well. Practically everything a child learns about spelling has direct or carry-over value to reading.

Psycholinguistics seems to hold potential for aiding the reading teacher. Surely the study of an area which promises an exploration of both *psyche* (the mind) and *linguistics* (language) must go right to the heart of many difficult and enduring problems. The term *psycholinguistics,* however, calls most readily to mind a confusing array of scientific, near-scientific, and outright pseudo-scientific theorizings concerning more the abnormal than the normal reading process. The academic journeyer into this area is likely to find himself lost in the never-never-land of dyslexia, minimal brain damage, cerebral dysfunction, and language-learning disability.

As one who works directly with children with severe reading problems, the writer has been particularly disappointed with the elaborate tests which purport to measure psycholinguistic abilities, and even more disappointed with the programs of therapy built around these and related tests.

Reading is a physical process exclusively—beginning, middle, and end. The reading teacher can continue to expect only limited practical assistance from the linguistic camp until the psychologist and the linguist who occupy it add a third member of their team. When it becomes neuropsycholinguistics, we may begin to hear reliable answers to straightforward questions about the reading process itself.

Both *lexicography,* the dictionary maker's number one tool, and its companion, *etymology,* that linguistic branch which attempts to trace out histories and origins of words, have been used directly by good reading teachers for a great many years. At its lowest level of usage, lexicography is a valuable and sophisticated word attack skill. (When all else fails, look the new or unfamiliar word up in the dictionary.) At its inspiring best, lexicography is one of the creative teacher's most direct answers to vocabulary enlargement and enrichment. I have known some children who read the dictionary for fun. Almost all of them have the capacity for genuine enjoyment in tracing out the histories of interesting words.

Once one has heard the story of Tantalus, who can forget the meaning of *tantalize?* Here are a half-dozen sure-fire winners: sabotage, taxicab, companion, abet, calculate, and infant.

Somewhere in my files is a list of a hundred or so words with interesting histories. I have found that all children seem to enjoy playing with a few of them. Some children find them a virtually endless source of delight.

If any branch of linguistics has a claim to the title of "potentially most important contributor to reading instruction," semantics is a chief contender. Semantics is the science of meaning in communication—and without meaning there is no reading. Probably nothing associated with reading instruction is more in need of a new, hard look than comprehension and the reading-study jobs. Good research in this area is scarce, indeed; what we have is largely out-of-date and inadequate.

Comprehension is the real challenge to linguistics. Beginning reading instruction, decoding, and word attack have all received generous contributions from linguistics. It is now comprehension's time—and none too soon. To begin, it would be nice to have a definitive analysis of the skills involved. It hardly seems possible that after years of teaching them, we are not at all sure what the real comprehension skills are.

Conclusions

Sixty or seventy years ago, when reading instruction was just emerging as a fit matter for academic concern at the normal college level, a fresh new discipline was evolving across campuses in the colleges of arts and sciences. The name of this discipline is psychology.

Immediately, scholars from both campuses saw the tremendous potential that the discoveries of the one held for the improvement of the other. Ergo, the psychological method of teaching reading was born. The psychology-reading relationship must have been exciting to our colleagues of fifty years ago. It is still exciting today.

But who would dare deliver a paper before the International Reading Association today on the topic "*The* Psychological Method of Reading Instruction" or "Psychological Programs of Reading Instruction, Are They Really Different?" What publisher would be foolish enough to advertise its program as being based on *the* psychological method of teaching reading? As a matter of course, we expect methods to be psychologically sound; and any program lacking psychological integrity is not long for this world. Talking about "*the* linguistic method" of reading instruction or "linguistic programs" of reading instruction is like talking about "*the* psychological method" of reading instruction or "psychological programs" of reading instruction—woefully out of date.

WHAT ARE THE "BEST" ANSWERS TO CLAIMS THAT AUDITORY-PERCEPTUAL DISCRIMINATION TRAINING AND VISUAL-PERCEPTUAL DISCRIMINATION TRAINING ARE SIGNIFICANT FACTORS IN BEGINNING READING?

HELEN M. ROBINSON (Professor Emeritus)
University of Chicago

provides an array of definitive answers gleaned from an extensive review of research.

PERCEPTUAL TRAINING—DOES IT RESULT IN READING IMPROVEMENT?

Teachers and researchers assume that one of the bases for learning to read is perceptual competence. Three major perceptual areas have been emphasized: visual, auditory, and kinaesthetic or tactual. A wide variety of approaches to the study of the first two areas—visual and auditory perception—have been attempted. Even though the evidence concerning the roles of these perceptual abilities has been less than clear, reading readiness tests have regularly included subtests relating especially to visual perception. Many of the programs designed to improve school or reading readiness have included exercises dealing with visual and auditory perception, and some have incorporated visual-motor skills.

Today, after more than thirty years of study, the question of the effects of perceptual training on learning to read is not answered. Some authorities and teachers are committed to perceptual training. Others are skeptical of its values and point to the contamination of instructional procedures which obscure the effects of perceptual training.

The purpose of this paper is to summarize the accumulated evidence supporting and rejecting the usefulness of perceptual training in increasing reading competency. In synthesizing the findings of studies, a number of unanswered questions are raised.

Terms Used

Before examining the evidence, it is necessary to specify the scope of the discussion. As Robinson (*35*) points out, even among educators terms must be defined in order to communicate.

Perception refers to the awareness of objects, relations, or qualities stimulated by the sense organs and influenced by set and prior experience.

Visual perception means the ability to perceive visual stimuli, particularly forms, letters, words, phrases, and sentences that are printed. It includes *discrimination,* the ability to differentiate one stimulus from another; *span,* the ability to recall *stimuli;* and *sequence,* the ability to keep the stimuli in some prearranged order.

Auditory perception includes the ability to perceive sounds, to differentiate one from another, to recall them, and to keep them in a prearranged order.

Visual and auditory perception, moreover, need to be associated and integrated in such a way that the child can successfully translate visual stimuli into spoken words or meaning.

Training embraces both the informal and formal (prescribed) procedures for developing competence in visual or auditory perceptions, audiovisual, motor, kinaesthetic, or any combination of these abilities.

Perceptual Training

In general, two types of procedures have been used to improve the reading of children classified as perceptually handicapped. The first type appears to relate primarily to attention or set. Using this type of procedure, teachers remove any environmental distractors. Children may be isolated in "neutral" areas. Only a line of print or a word or letter may be shown, surrounded by open space; and children are given cues to expect particular stimuli. Those who show auditory distractions may use earphones to exclude noise from the environment, and it is possible to increase the intensity of the sound of the teacher's voice by using an appropriate instrument. Little or no research has been found to support these techniques.

The second type of approach involves instruction directed toward the improvement of a particular deficit. Such activities as tracing, copying with and without the stimulus in view, choosing a correct stimulus among several, and naming digits, forms, or words have been tried. To improve auditory perception, exercises similar to those found in auditory perception tests are most common. In addition, a variety of motor and visual-motor activities ranging from Kephart's balance board to tracing monocular forms in a binocular instrument have been reported.

Myriad claims and counterclaims have been made concerning the relative values of each type of perceptual-training procedure: first, for retarded readers; second, as a means of preventing reading failure; and, third, to improve the reading of all children.

Perceptually handicapped children are often assigned to special classes, particularly in the primary grades. Both reports and observations reveal that the means for identifying pupils to be assigned to such classes vary markedly. The types of training given are equally divergent, and the means for evaluating the effectiveness of perceptual training range from observation of individual pupil's behavior to controlled studies of individuals and groups in which evaluative instruments are quite different.

Visual Perception

As long ago as the mid 20s, Gates (*18*) experimented with various tests and reported that his findings supported the conclusion that visual-perceptual ability is not a unitary factor but that it has many facets. Further, he found that perception involving letters, syllables, and words was more closely related to reading achievement than the nonword forms. The implication from this and many subsequent studies is that visual-perception training should use words as targets.

In the next decades visual-perception training became synonymous with word perception. Meanwhile, the Thurstones (*43*) were exploring the relationship of perceptual measures both to reading and to intelligence. Indeed, Thelma G. Thurstone* prepared a series of books to help young children develop their primary mental abilities with significant emphasis on visual perception. Teachers who wished to instruct children specifically in visual-perceptual abilities had little else to guide them at that time.

Tachistoscopic Training and Reading Achievement

A new wave of experimentation came after Renshaw (*34*) reported that speed and accuracy of aircraft recognition could be achieved with tachistoscopic training. Subsequently, he reported reading improvement, first among adults and then among children, as a result of rapid recognition of digits. A number of school people then began to use tachistoscopic training.

In 1958, however, Goins (*19*) equated two groups of first grade children in each of two schools on the basis of intelligence quotients, reading achievements, and total scores on 14 visual-perception tests. The experimental group received tachistoscopic training with designs

* *The Red Book, The Blue Book,* and *The Green Book.* Chicago: Science Research Associates.

and digits; some letters and short words were added near the end of the period. The training was given three days each week for ten weeks. Meanwhile, the control group continued their usual classroom activities. Retesting revealed that the experimental group was better able to perceive digits adequately than the control group but that the reading achievement of the two groups did not differ.

Subsequently, other investigators used tachistoscopic training for beginners, generally without evidence of improvement in reading. An exception is reported in the more recent study by Wheelock and Silvaroli (*46*) who trained kindergarten children of high and low socioeconomic levels on instant discrimination of capital letters. The men used no naming or sounding of letters so that the training was visual perceptual in nature. Teachers, however, analyzed the differences between letters for the pupils. The experimental group scored significantly higher than the control group on the letter forms and on subtests of the Lee-Clark Reading Readiness Test. The authors report that children in the lower socioeconomic levels benefited most by the training. Whether such improvement in measures of visual perception would transfer to reading was not established, nor was the effect of the teachers' guidance considered.

Olson (*32*) trained first grade subjects on 14 known words using the tachistoscopic procedure and found that errors increased significantly with speed of exposure. He concluded "that tachistoscopic work on sight vocabulary words may not be a learning reinforcement task at first grade level."

Frostig Materials and Reading Achievement

Another procedure for improving visual perception was devised by Frostig (*17*) and has been used by a number of investigators. Fortenberry (*15*) used it with culturally disadvantaged children for 12 weeks. No significant improvement on measures of visual perception was found. However, performance on one subtest of the Gates Primary Reading Test was significantly higher for the experimental group after 12 weeks; but by the end of 24 weeks that superiority had disappeared. The Frostig program had been of no lasting value to reading competence.

After 29 days of training with the Frostig materials, Rosen (*37*) found that the trained group was superior to the untrained group on Frostig's tests, but there were no comparable gains in reading achievement. In fact, the control group surpassed the trained group on two other tests.

Even when the program is introduced at kindergarten, and in the first or second half of first grade, Jacobs, et al (*21*) found higher scores on the readiness test for subjects trained with the Frostig materials but no significant difference in reading in first grade. By second grade, the control group even exceeded the experimental group.

It might be argued that using whole classes of pupils masks the effect of the program on children who score low on the Frostig tests. But Cohen (*5*) trained only those first graders who scored low on the Frostig test and found no reading improvement that could be attributed to the perceptual training.

Balow (*1*) states that Buckland trained first grade pupils scoring low on reading readiness tests, using the Frostig workbooks. After 40 periods of 15 minutes each, there was no difference between experimental and control groups. A comparison of those who scored lowest on the initial Frostig test shows that the control group far surpassed the trained children, an outcome which suggests that listening to stories produces better reading progress than does the Frostig program.

The foregoing reports strongly suggest that the Frostig program of visual-perceptual training is not effective in improving reading regardless of the school level at which it is introduced, the number of periods of instruction, the socioeconomic level of the pupils, or the scores the pupils make on initial visual-perceptual tests.

Physical Coordination Training and Reading Achievement

A third type of training which was devised by Kephart and his associates (*4*) emphasizes physical coordination and eye-hand coordination as a means of improving visual perception and reading. McBeath (*28*) used this program, as well as the Frostig program, with kindergarten children. Neither program alone nor the alternation of the two programs significantly improved reading readiness as it was measured by the Lee-Clark test or as observed by teachers using a schedule. Rutherford (*38*) also used the Kephart procedure at kindergarten level and, in contrast to the McBeath findings, reports that boys, especially, improved on the Metropolitan Readiness Test as a result of training.

An adaptation of the Kephart program, combined with some aspects of the Winter Haven program, was used by Faustman (*13*) in kindergarten. No significant improvement was shown by the trained group on the Winter Haven Perceptual Ability Forms Test at the end of kindergarten. However, in both November and May of first grade, the trained group was superior to the control group in reading. Bosworth (*3*) found marked improvement in copying forms on an adaptation of the Winter Haven test after kindergarten training with this program. In addition, scores on the Betts Word-Form Test reflected the training of the visual-motor skills.

In contrast, Keim (*25*) trained only the kindergarten children who demonstrated deficiencies in visual-motor abilities. His results show no positive effects of the Winter Haven training program on performance on the Metropolitan Readiness Test.

Other Visual Perceptual Training Programs and Reading Achievement

A number of other types of programs have been tried in an effort to improve visual perception and reading. Lloyd (*27*) gave the Howard-Dolman test twice each week for three months with little or no positive effect on reading. A combination of gross motor eye-hand coordination, form perception, and spatial relationships in kindergarten was compared to the effects of the regular kindergarten program. No significant effects of the perceptual program on reading readiness were found at the end of kindergarten, nor was there any difference in reading scores at the middle of second grade. Falik (*12*) raised serious questions about his measuring instruments for studies of this kind.

Visual discrimination of abstract symbols was compared to training in discriminating meaningful symbols before reading was taught in first grade. Although Gorelick (*20*) found no differences between the groups at the end of ten days of instruction, the group taught with abstract symbols was better in delayed recall than the one taught with meaningful symbols, but no better than the control group.

At second grade, Elkind and Deblinger (*10*) introduced nonverbal perceptual training for disadvantaged pupils. The control group used the Bank Street Readers. After 45 one-half hour sessions, children given perceptual training scored higher than those in the control group on a test of word recognition. Discrimination of letter-like forms, which include rotations and reversals, proved to be more effective than discrimination of dissimilar words, according to Williams (*47*).

Space orientation appeared to be the major deficit among retarded readers treated by Silver and Hagin (*39*). Furthermore, from ten to over fifty hours of visual-perceptual training were needed for these pupils to learn to recognize, copy, and recall even simple geometric forms. Of special interest here is the conclusion that, as these children grew to adulthood, the defects lessened but did not completely disappear.

The foregoing studies of the relationship of training in visual perception to reading achievement leads to no clear-cut conclusions. In general, this training results in improvement on tests of visual perception but seldom is resultant reading improvement, if any, substantial or lasting. Even the few early gains reported seem to disappear by second or third grade. Moreover, concerning reading disabilities, Balow (*1*) states that no acceptable studies support the effectiveness of physical, motor, or perceptual programs, either in preventing or correcting reading disabilities.

Unresolved Questions

A number of pertinent questions are still unanswered: Have the tests of visual perception been adequately developed to identify all aspects essential to reading? Investigations of the Frostig test, for example (*26, 33*), cast doubt on its transfer and/or predictive value for reading competence. Do all children improve in visual perception if given proper training, or only those who are deficient? Is visual-perceptual deficiency due to lack of experience, to inattention, to some neurological deficit, to immaturity, or to some unidentified factor? If the major problem is immaturity, will improvement occur spontaneously through maturation alone? If so, could some of the results now claimed for training be a result of maturation? Finally, is there some minimum level of visual perception which facilitates learning to read, above which there is no added advantage to further competence by special visual-perceptual training?

Auditory Perception

Fewer studies of treatment to improve auditory discrimination have been located. Using a number of classes in three schools, Duggins (*7*) introduced auditory training at the beginning of first grade, in the middle of the first year, and in second grade. At the end of second grade, the group that had received auditory-perceptual training in first grade averaged five months above the control group in reading achievement.

A tape recorded program based on Durrell's Building Word Power was the treatment offered to an experimental group of third grade pupils by Evans (*11*). She developed 40 segments, each of 15 minutes' duration, to be administered daily. Auditory discrimination was improved significantly through the training, and there was a corresponding improvement in oral reading. Pupils with poorer auditory-discrimination scores on the pretest made the greatest gains on post-tests of auditory discrimination.

The same pattern of auditory-discrimination difficulties was found among upper and lower socioeconomic groups by Jeffares and Cosens (*22*). The degree of deficit, however, was greater among children of lower socioeconomic levels. Auditory-discrimination training, using word-pair exercises, was provided for half of the first grade subjects with lower initial scores. After ten minutes of daily training for a month, there was significant improvement in all types of subjects comprising the experimental group. There was no comparable difference, however, in oral or silent reading. The fact that this training was given in May and June at the end of first grade, may have depressed the effects on reading.

Deutsch and Feldman (*6*) treated disadvantaged retarded readers in the primary grades for deficiencies in auditory discrimination. The treatments involved auditory training only, reading instruction only, and successive or combined reading and auditory training. In both of their studies, there was no evidence that auditory-perceptual training improved reading achievement.

Auditory-perception training of the types used so far has not demonstrated any conclusive effect on reading competence. The same types of unanswered questions as those suggested on visual perception could be posed about auditory. Pertinent to the solution of these problems are the conclusions of Dykstra (*9*) who discovered that different relationships are found among various tests of auditory discrimination and different reading tests, even with the same population. Since the precise auditory abilities or combination of abilities has not been identified, training still remains a global kind of program.

In his attempts to improve auditory discrimination and memory among children with speech defects, Wepman found spontaneous improvement equal to that achieved by training. Consequently, he ascribes much of the deficiency in auditory perception to late maturation and notes that some children do not acquire adequate auditory abilities until the eighth year of life (*45*). Thus the problem of the effectiveness of auditory-perceptual training remains unsolved.

Visual and Auditory Training

In many instances, visual- and auditory-perceptual training have been instituted simultaneously. Sometimes the training has been preliminary to reading; other times it has been concurrent with reading instruction.

In an attempt to improve visual and auditory discriminations, Skinner (*40*) provided one group with visual discrimination and auditory discrimination exercises that were unrelated. This treatment proved to be superior to one which combined visual and auditory trainings when post-tests of visual discrimination were given. However, no difference was found on tests of auditory discrimination.

Training in sequential repetition of names of pictures of common objects, digits, and colors was given by Fillmer and Linder (*14*). Presentations were auditory, visual, and auditory-visual on each type of materials. Second grade Black boys of low socioeconomic level were asked to recall the sets of stimuli in sequence. The investigators found that recall of the auditory presentations was distinctly inferior to the visual or auditory visual in two of the three tasks and equal to it in the third. The visual presentations proved to be equal to the auditory visual in the learning produced.

The studies of auditory-visual integration by Kahn and Birch (*24*) show that pupils who scored low or high on integration tests had equally intact visual and auditory perception. The researchers conclude, therefore, that the integration of the perceptual abilities really made the difference in the two groups.

In one of the twenty-seven USOE Cooperative Studies of first grade reading, Spache and his associates (*41*) made extensive use of training in visual, visual-motor, and auditory perception to improve reading readiness. They found that their program was more effective with Black than with White children who scored low on the reading readiness tests. However, instruction in other areas, such as language, and the delay of formal reading instruction contaminated the effects of the visual and auditory training in the Spache study.

Effects of Reading Instruction on Perceptual Discrimination

An indefinite distinction may be found between training in visual and auditory perception and reading instruction, especially when letters and words are targets. Some investigators, such as Durrell (*8*), contend that reading instruction itself improves visual and auditory perception. Murphy (*30*) demonstrates the superiority of teaching the names and sounds of letters, compared to the readiness program of a basal series, in terms of later reading achievement.

As to the best sequence of teaching letter names and sounds in relation to words, Myers (*31*) finds that children who scored average on reading readiness tests learn to read better if the letter names and sounds are taught prior to teaching words. Initial instruction in letter names only produced better results, however, with children not ready to read. Visual discrimination training with four letter words was found to be superior to training using the separate letters that make up the words (*42*).

Children who had tactile training learned four words easier than those who rearranged letters to match a word or chose the matching word among foils (*23*). Among six approaches to learning words, Muehl and King (*29*) conclude that hearing words pronounced is most effective when the words are dissimilar; but when they are similar, the addition of pictures and other cues is most effective.

Assuming that tests can identify serious deficits in visual or auditory perception, two opposing procedures are recommended to reduce failure in learning to read. One proposes to choose an instructional approach that makes primary use of intact perceptual abilities. The other proposes training in the deficit area prior to reading instruction, in view of the fact that both types of perceptual abilities are essential to reading.

Two investigations attempted to determine the effects of using weak and strong perceptual abilities in teaching reading. Bateman (*2*) identified audile and visile learners in first grade by comparing two subtests on the Illinois Test of Psycholinguistic Abilities. Her means for making the comparisons for identifying the two types of learners have been seriously questioned. Nevertheless, she provided reading instruction to half of each group while emphasizing their strong perceptual area. To the other half, instruction made use primarily of their weak area. At the end of first grade, both audile and visile children taught by an auditory approach made greater improvement in reading than those taught by a visual approach.

In a study which is not yet published, Robinson (*36*) located four school systems, two of which began by teaching phonics and the other two began with sight words. It was reasoned that poor auditory and good visual-perceptual ability would predispose greater facility in learning by a sight approach, while good auditory and poor visual-perceptual ability would result in greater gains in reading by a phonic approach.

At the end of both first and third grades, neither method consistently proved to be more effective than the other in compensating for inadequacies in perceptual types. The question of the dependability of perceptual tests limits the conclusions reached from this study, too.

Summary

The research shows no conclusive answers to the question of the effectiveness of perceptual training to improve reading. While some programs appear to improve perceptual performance in the areas trained, the long-term effect on reading is uncertain. Nor is it clear whether the usual program of reading instruction may, in itself, include crucial elements which result in improved scores on perceptual tests.

The role of experience, motivation, and personal qualities may account for some of the reported gains. From an extensive analysis of the research on visual perception Vernon (*44*) concludes that the main effects of motivation, set, and the like are indirect, resulting in different pupils' acquiring different types of knowledge and skills. In turn, these experiences set up certain schemata which direct selective attention along particular lines. Thus, it may be possible that scores on perceptual tests result, in part, from selective attention.

The role of attention is underscored by Frantz (*16*) who found that, within the first three months of life, infants can respond selectively to patterns presented visually. Thereafter, looking becomes a guide to oral, manual, and locomotor activities, but, later, interest returns to patterns. He states that "Changes in visual selectivity may, in fact, be of more critical importance, in that the basic oculomotor coordinations, visual acuities, and pattern-discrimination capacities are present long before they are put to use in deciphering markings on paper—a conclusion of the recent research—is the strong influence of selective attention to patterns in general—during the earliest stage of perceptual development." Perhaps it will be necessary to determine the extent to which children possess perceptual abilities and the possibility that these abilities are focused on nonreading activities before the problem of training is solved.

Prior to reaching definitive conclusions, it will be necessary to develop sensitive measures of the aspects of perception which are essential to reading competence. As Balow (*1*) points out, such weaknesses of perceptual development (as are now recognized) may simply be concomitants without causal relevance, and a number of other factors may actually be responsible for the gains in reading now ascribed to visual- and/or auditory-perceptual training.

References

1. Balow, Bruce. "Perceptual-Motor Activities in the Treatment of Severe Reading Disability," *Reading Teacher,* 24 (March 1971), 513-525, 542.

2. Bateman, Barbara. "The Efficacy of an Auditory and a Visual Method of First Grade Reading Instruction with Auditory and Visual Learners," in Helen K. Smith (Ed.), *Perception and Reading,* 1967 Proceedings, Volume 12, Part 4. Newark, Delaware: International Reading Association, 1968, 105-112.

3. Bosworth, Mary H. "Prereading: Improvement of Visual-Motor Skills," doctoral dissertation, University of Miami, 1967.

4. Chaney, Clara, and Newell Kephart. *Motoric Aids to Perceptual Training.* Columbus: Merrill, 1968.

5. Cohen, Ruth Isenberg. "Remedial Training of First Grade Children with Visual Perceptual Retardation," *Educational Horizons,* 45 (Winter 1966), 60-63.

6. Deutsch, Cynthia P., and Shirley C. Feldman. "A Study of the Effectiveness of Training for Retarded Readers in the Auditory Skills Underlying Reading," Title VII Project No. 1127 Grant, U.S. Department of Health, Education and Welfare, Office of Education, Institute for Developmental Studies, New York Medical College, 1966.

7. Duggins, Lydia A. "Experimental Studies in Auditory Perception in Beginning Reading," *Auditory Perception in the Beginning Reading Program,* College Bulletin, Southeastern Louisiana College, 13 (January 1956), 12-18.

8. Durrell, Donald D. "First-Grade Reading Success Study: A Summary," *Journal of Education,* 140 (February 1958), 2-6.

9. Dykstra, Robert. "Auditory Discrimination Abilities and Beginning Reading Achievement," *Reading Research Quarterly,* 1 (Spring 1966), 9-34.

10. Elkind, D., and Jo Ann Deblinger. "Perceptual Training and Reading Achievement in Disadvantaged Children," *Child Development,* 40 (March 1969), 11-19.

11. Evans, Jackie Merion. "The Development of Auditory Discrimination in Third Grade Students by Use of Tape Recorded Materials," doctoral dissertation, North Texas State University, 1965.

12. Falik, Louis H. "The Effects of Special Perceptual-Motor Training in

Kindergarten on Reading Readiness and on Second Grade Reading Performance," *Journal of Learning Disabilities,* 2 (August 1969), 395-402.

13. Faustman, Marion N. "Some Effects of Perception Training in Kindergarten on First Grade Success in Reading," in Helen K. Smith (Ed.), *Perception and Reading,* 1967 Proceedings, Volume 12, Part 4. Newark, Delaware: International Reading Association 1968, 99-101.
14. Fillmer, Henry T., and Ronald Linder. "Comparison of Auditory and Visual Modalities," *Education,* 91 (November-December 1970), 110-113.
15. Fortenberry, Warren D. "An Investigation of the Effectiveness of a Special Program upon the Development of Visual Perception for Word Recognition of Culturally Disadvantaged First Grade Students," in George B. Schick and Merrill May (Eds.), *Reading: Process and Pedagogy,* Nineteenth Yearbook of the National Reading Conference, Volume I. Milwaukee: National Reading Conference, 1970, 141-145.
16. Frantz, Robert L. "Visual Perception and Experience in Infancy: Issues and Approaches," in Francis A. Young and Donald B. Linsley (Eds.), *Early Experience and Visual Information Processing in Perceptual and Reading Disorder.* Washington, D.C.: National Academy of Sciences, 1970, 351-381.
17. Frostig, Marianne, and David Horne. *The Frostig Program for the Development of Visual Perception: Teacher's Guide.* Chicago: Follett, 1964.
18. Gates, Arthur I. "A Study of the Role of Visual Perception, Intelligence and Certain Associative Processes in Reading and Spelling," *Journal of Educational Psychology,* 17 (October 1926), 433-445.
19. Goins, Jean Turner. *Visual Perceptual Abilities and Early Reading Progress,* Supplementary Educational Monographs, No. 87. Chicago: University of Chicago Press, 1958.
20. Gorelick, Molly C. "The Effectiveness of Visual Form Training in a Prereading Program," *Journal of Educational Research,* 58 (March 1965), 315-318.
21. Jacobs, J. N., Lenore D. Wirthlin, and C. B. Miller. "A Follow-Up Evaluation of the Frostig-Visual Perceptual Training Program," *Educational Leadership,* 26 (November 1968), 169-175.
22. Jeffares, Dolores J., and Grace V. Cosene. "Effects of Socioeconomic Status and Auditory Discrimination Training on First Grade Reading Achievement and Auditory Discrimination," *Alberta Journal of Educational Research,* 16 (September 1970), 165-178.

23. Jensen, Norma J., and Ethel M. King. "Effects of Different Kinds of Visual-Motor Discrimination Training on Learning to Read Words," *Journal of Educational Psychology,* 61 (April 1970), 90-96.
24. Kahn, D., and H. G. Birch. "Development of Auditory-Visual Integration and Reading Achievement," *Perceptual and Motor Skills,* 27 (October 1968), 459-468.
25. Keim, Richard P. "Visual-Motor Training, Readiness, and Intelligence of Kindergarten Children," *Journal of Learning Disabilities,* 3 (May 1970), 19-22.
26. Leibert, Robert E., and John Sherk. "Three Frostig Visual Perception Subtests and Specific Reading Tasks for Kindergarten, First, and Second Grade Children," *Reading Teacher,* 24 (November 1970), 130-137.
27. Lloyd, Bruce. "The Effects of Programmed Perceptual Training on the Reading Achievement and Mental Maturity of Selected First Grade Pupils: A Pilot Study," *Journal of the Reading Specialist,* 6 (December 1966), 49-55.
28. McBeath, Pearl Marcia Loebenstein. "The Effectiveness of Three Reading Preparedness Programs for Perceptually Handicapped Kindergartners," doctoral dissertation, Stanford University, 1966.
29. Muehl, Sigmar, and Ethel M. King. "Recent Research in Visual Discrimination: Significance for Beginning Reading," in J. Allen Figurel (Ed.), *Vistas in Reading,* 1966 Proceedings, Volume 11, Part 1. Newark, Delaware: International Reading Association, 1967, 434-439.
30. Murphy, Helen A. "A Research Pitfall: Jumping to Conclusions," in J. Allen Figurel (Ed.), *Challenge and Experiment in Reading,* Proceedings of the International Reading Association, 7, 1962. New York: Scholastic Magazines, 117-119.
31. Myers, Dorothy Charlotte. "The Effects of Letter Knowledge on Achievement in Reading in the First Grade," doctoral dissertation, University of Missouri at Columbia, 1966.
32. Olson, Arthur V. "Cues in Word Perception in Relation to Osgood's Integration Principle," in George D. Spache (Ed.), *Reading Disability and Perception,* 1968 Proceedings, Volume 13, Part 3. Newark, Delaware: International Reading Association, 1969, 117.
33. Olson, Arthur V., and Clifford I. Johnson. "Structure and Predictive Validity of the Frostig Developmental Test of Visual Perception in Grades One and Three," *Journal of Special Education,* 4 (Winter-Spring 1970), 49-52.

34. Renshaw, Samuel. "The Visual Perception and Reproduction of Forms by Tachistoscopic Methods," *Journal of Psychology,* 20 (October 1945), 217-232.
35. Robinson, Helen M. "Significant Unsolved Problems in Reading," *Journal of Reading,* 14 (November 1970), 77-82, 134-141.
36. Robinson, Helen M. "Visual and Auditory Modalities Related to Two Methods for Beginning Reading," unpublished study.
37. Rosen, Carl L. "An Experimental Study of Visual Perceptual Training and Reading Achievement in First Grade," *Perceptual and Motor Skills,* 22 (June 1966), 979-986.
38. Rutherford, W. L. "Perceptual-Motor Training and Readiness," in J. Allen Figurel (Ed.), *Reading and Inquiry,* Proceedings, 10. Newark, Delaware: International Reading Association, 1965, 294-296.
39. Silver, Archie A., and Rosa A. Hagin. "Visual Perception in Children with Reading Disabilities," in Francis A. Young and Donald B. Linsley (Eds.), *Early Experience and Visual Information Processing in Perceptual and Reading Disorders.* Washington, D.C.: National Academy of Sciences, 1970, 445-456.
40. Skinner, Georgieann Tuech. "Single Versus Multiple Modality in Visual and Auditory Discrimination Training," doctoral dissertation, Arizona State University, 1968.
41. Spache, G. D., et al. "A Longitudinal First Grade Reading Readiness Program," *Reading Teacher,* 19 (May 1966), 580-584.
42. Staats, Carolyn K., Arthur W. Staats, and Richard E. Schultz. "The Effects of Discrimination Pretraining on Textual Behavior," *Journal of Educational Psychology,* 53 (February 1962), 32-37.
43. Thurstone, L. L., and Thelma Gwinn Thurstone. "Factorial Studies of Intelligence," *Psychometric Monographs,* No. 2. Chicago: University of Chicago Press, 1941.
44. Vernon, M. D. *Perception through Experience.* New York: Barnes and Nobel, 1970.
45. Wepman, Joseph M. "Modalities and Learning" in Helen M. Robinson (Ed.), *Coordinating Reading Instruction.* Glenview, Illinois: Scott, Foresman, 1971, 55-60.
46. Wheelock, Warren H., and Nicholas J. Silvaroli. "An Investigation of Visual Discrimination Training for Beginning Readers," *Journal of Typographic Research,* 1 (April 1967), 147-156.
47. Williams, Joanna P. "Training Kindergarten Children to Discriminate Letter-Like Forms," *American Educational Research Journal,* 6 (November 1969), 501-513.

48. Young, Francis A., and Donald B. Linsley. *Early Experience and Visual Information Processing in Perceptual and Reading Disorders.* Washington, D.C.: National Academy of Sciences, 1970.

Stephen E. Klesius
University of South Florida

presents a refinement of a prior report to the College Reading Association and provides some answers.

PERCEPTUAL-MOTOR DEVELOPMENT AND READING—A CLOSER LOOK

Since the early sixties programs of perceptual-motor development have been used for various purposes in schools and clinics across the country. In addition, there is an ever-increasing amount of research being completed by reading, special education, early childhood, and physical education specialists. Research investigating the value of perceptual-motor programs would be more advantageous if compilation of those studies and their implications for educational programing were more readily available to administrators and teachers.

An earlier paper (*6*) reviewed 28 research studies that investigated the effectiveness of programs of perceptual-motor development upon reading readiness or upon the reading achievement of intellectually able students. The main conclusions of that review are:

> The effectiveness of perceptual-motor development programs in improving reading ability can neither be confirmed nor denied. In general, perceptual-motor programs employing a wide variety of experiences appear to show promise with underachieving, intermediate grade students, and preschool children. The effectiveness of Delacato and Frostig-type programs is doubtful.

Criteria

A question arises as to whether the conclusions would differ if only research of the highest quality had been considered for inclusion in the review. In an attempt to answer this question, criteria defining limits of acceptability for research to be reported were established. These criteria were applied to the studies reviewed in the previously cited paper and also to more recent research. It was hoped that this procedure would avoid basing conclusions on the inadequacies which characterize a large portion of the research pertaining to this topic.

The research studies accepted for inclusion in this review met the following criterion measures:

1. The studies must incorporate programs of perceptual-motor development comprising a wide variety of movement-based experiences which require accurate sensory interpretation to perform tasks ranging from large muscle locomotor patterns to precise, fine muscle coordination. (Accordingly the limited perceptual-motor development activity approaches of Delacato, the Winter Haven Program, and Frostig prior to 1970 when used independently of other perceptual-motor development activities were excluded from this review.)
2. The studies must include a minimum of at least 40 subjects, equally divided between the control and experimental groups.
3. An experimental period of one-half of a school year (18 weeks) was considered the minimum length for inclusion in this study. In addition a postinvestigation followup of the subjects' achievements was included as an extra measure. These data would indicate retention of gains or effects accrued after the termination of the special program.
4. A pre/post test research design with experimental and control groups was deemed desirable to account for changes possibly occurring as a result of maturation, regular instruction, or special effects. Several studies failed to include a pretest but were reported because of high ratings on the other criterion measures.
5. Reasonable control of intervening variables was also sought in the studies accepted. Some researchers would insist on rigorous control which is extremely difficult in applied research in school settings.
6. The utilization of proper statistical analysis of the data and conclusions based on the attained results were included in the criteria. Occasionally inappropriate statistical analysis is used, and more frequently conclusions reflect conscious or unconscious bias.

Research Findings

From a total of 38 studies investigating the influence of perceptual-motor development programs upon reading, 11 studies rated high enough on the review criteria to warrant a closer look. The studies are presented according to whether they support or reject the hypothesis that programs of perceptual-motor development enhance reading readiness or achievement of intellectually able students. (For the purpose of this paper an intellectually able student is nonmentally retarded.)

Studies Supporting the Hypothesis

A physiology of readiness experiment through perceptual-motor training was conducted by McCulloch (*8*) for the Ripon Wisconsin Public School system. Two kindergarten classes were selected to participate in the study which lasted 18 weeks. One class received 30 minutes of perceptual-motor training plus 10 to 20 minutes of selected Frostig materials daily while the other class was used as control subjects. The students were pre- and post-tested, using measures of visual perception, mental ability, and readiness skills. Analysis of the data reveals that the experimental group made significantly greater gains than did the control group on the Metropolitan Readiness Test. No significant differences between the groups were found on their performances on the Otis-Lemon Mental Ability Test or on the Gates-MacGinitie Readiness Skill Test. The hypothesis that readiness can be systematically developed on a physiological basis was accepted.

In a study using 76 culturally disadvantaged kindergarten children as subjects, Turner and Fisher (*17*) conclude that ". . . intensive exposure to verbal concepts, paired with concrete examples and movement, may have been a major program effect in enhancing reading readiness." In this study Kephart-type activities were incorporated in the experimental kindergarten program which was conducted for two hours per day for seven months. Possible criticism of this study is based on the fact that the Metropolitan Readiness Test and the Purdue Perceptual-Motor Survey were given only at the end of the study.

The New Jersey State Department of Education (*11*) conducted a longitudinal study of 275 primary grade children during a three year period. The subjects were matched except that the experimental subjects were one year behind the control subjects in reading. The experimental group received a perceptual-motor development program in addition to regular school instruction. After one year the control group continued to perform significantly higher on academic tests. At the end of the second and third years no significant differences between the two groups were found. The subjects receiving perceptual-motor training "appeared to have the faster growth rate." Slower children seemed to have benefited from the special training whereas the other children generally had not. The measurement instruments consisted of the California Achievement Test, the Gates Reading Test, and the Metropolitan Readiness Test.

Weisman and Leonard (*18*) used a multidisciplinary approach in an attempt to develop verbal and reading skills of low socioeconomic level children. A team consisting of a physical education specialist, a social worker, and a classroom teacher worked with 20 students selected at random to be in the experimental group from the middle of kindergarten through the first grade. Perceptual-motor-development activities based on the work of Cratty, Frostig, Kephart, and others were a major part of the physical education program which, in general, met for 30 minutes daily during the experimental period. Development in areas such as balance, body image, ocular control, and perception of figure-ground relationship was stressed because it was believed they were "important prerequisites to learning to read."

The first phase of the study did not employ statistical comparison, but it was reported that the experimental subjects performed at higher levels than did the students in the control group on the Bettye Caldwell Preschool Inventory Expressive Verbal Test; on the verbal section of the Primary Mental Abilities Test, and on the tests accompanying the SRA Reading Program. Moreover, after a period of one year, and without additional special instruction, the students who completed the multidisciplinary program including perceptual-motor development training still scored significantly higher on the Primary Reading Profile Test—Level I than did the 20 subjects who had not received that perceptual-motor training.

A study by Faustman (*4*) involving 200 children was conducted to determine the effect of perceptual training in kindergarten upon first grade success in reading. The experimental treatment included Frostig, Strauss, and Kephart perceptual-motor activities. Differences between groups were found for form perception at kindergarten and first grade level. No difference in reading as measured by the Gates Word Recognition Test was found at the end of kindergarten. The experimental group, however, was superior in reading ability on tests given in November and May of the first school year. It was concluded that the greater gains for the experimental group could be attributed to the effect of the perceptual-motor training in kindergarten.

In summary, three of the studies were done using students who were behind in reading or were from low socioeconomic environments. The remaining two studies had as subjects children who were attending kindergarten. Several of the studies had special treatment influences operating in addition to perceptual-motor programs. The studies were those of Turner and Fisher (*11*) and Weisman and Leonard (*18*). In addition, McCulloch's study (*8*) found significantly greater gains on the Metropolitan Readiness Tests but not on the Gates-MacGinitie Readiness Skills Test. The latter test is the more extensive of the two and includes measures of auditory discrimination, following directions, and auditory blending.

Studies Rejecting the Hypothesis

Fisher (*5*) studies the effect of two types of physical education programs upon motor-skill development and on academic readiness of two groups of kindergarten children receiving the same instructional program. One group participated in a traditional game-type physical education program while the other participated in individualized perceptual-motor-development activities during physical education periods. Each program was conducted for 20 minutes per day, five times a week, for 22 weeks. The results on a motor ability test, a general intelligence test, and a general readiness test showed no significant differences between groups.

A Kephart-type program of perceptual-motor activities resulting in significant differences in internal awareness but not in perceptual ability, reading readiness, or achievement for first graders was done by O'Connor (*12*). His study extended for six months during first grade for 59 male and 64 female students. The special-treatment group received perceptual-motor activities, and the control group participated in traditional physical education activities. "The conclusion drawn from this study is that change in gross motor ability elicited by the Kephart-type gross motor activities does not necessarily effect change in perceptual ability nor in academic ability of the average first grader."

Slacks (*15*) conducted a program almost replicating O'Connor's study, wherein 54 first grade students received the perceptual-motor activities advocated by Kephart while 48 students participated in regular physical education activities. The programs lasted for 6 months and both groups (4 classes) received similar classroom instruction. The Perceptual Forms Test, Metropolitan Readiness Test, Metropolitan Achievement Test, teacher ratings, and overall academic performance were used as measures. The finding that there was no difference between group performances on the test measures was essentially the same as O'Connor's (*12*).

Primary level children identified as having learning disabilities were subjects in a study by Litchfield (7) that utilized visual-motor-perceptual activities with 80 first, second, and third grade students over a six-month period, with half-hour sessions each school day. Data were obtained from a fine-screening instrument, the Lorge-Thorndike Intelligence Test, the Stanford Achievement Test, and the Gates-MacGinitie Reading Test. No significant differences were revealed by statistical analysis for intelligence and achievement measures.

A program of body management, incorporating a diverse range of perceptual-motor activities, was reported by Braley (*1*). It was a longitudinal research study conducted in the Dayton, Ohio, Public School System to determine the effect of perceptual-motor training on four-year-old children and its influence, if any, on school achievement at the end of the first grade. An experimental sample of 65 children received experiences including body image, basic body movement, eye-hand and eye-foot coordination, form perception, and rhythms. A matched control sample received similar educational experiences but did not participate in the systematic perceptual-motor development program. The findings indicate that the perceptual-motor program enhanced prekindergarten and prefirst grade perceptual-motor performance to a significantly greater degree than did unstructured maturation. At the end of first grade, the experimental group showed significantly greater achievement on tests of auditory discrimination but not on reading.

One hundred and eight children in the primary grades who received regular school instruction plus one physical activity program—free play, perceptual-motor, traditional physical education, or adaptive physical education—were studied by McRaney (*10*). The length of the study was 20 weeks, and the subjects received 35-minute periods of the specified physical activities daily. Pre/post testing consisted of the Metropolitan Readiness Test, the Metropolitan Achievement Test, and the Purdue Perceptual-Motor Survey. No significant differences were found between the groups' perceptual-motor abilities, mental abilities, or educational achievements.

A summarization of the studies refuting the hypothesis reveal that 83 percent of the studies were with kindergarten or primary grade children who, in general, were not experiencing learning disabilities.

Of the five studies that included measures of perceptual-motor ability, only two find significantly greater improvement in perceptual-motor ability for the experimental group when compared to the control group and none of the studies finds any concomitant increase in reading achievement. These findings are contrary to claims made for such programs.

Conclusions

Programs of perceptual-motor development appear to be *developmentally* appropriate in view of the writings of authorities in child development (*3, 9*), child psychology (*13*), and visual perception (*14, 16*). But research indicates the case claiming that perceptual-motor development enhances reading achievement has been overstated.

Is this inaccuracy because perceptual-motor development programs at present are frequently given after the critical period in the developmental progression has past? Could it be that the reliance upon statistical analysis which is based on group data is misleading, and a closer look should be given to individual case studies and clinical evidence? Or could it be that a common neurological factor does *not* underly both perceptual-motor and reading achievement, and a better way to teach reading is to teach letters and words and to do it thoroughly (*2*). The answer to these questions can only come from additional research.

Perceptual-motor experiences have a place in physical education, day care, early childhood, and primary education. Perceptual-motor experiences should emphasize sequential development of a repertoire of neuromuscular skills which allow the individual to understand his body schema, discover his movement potentialities, develop efficient postural and locomotor patterns, and act with an accurate motoric response based on appropriately integrated input from the sensory milieu. The desired outcomes of enhanced movement efficiency and physical self-concept are more likely to occur as a result of developmentally sequenced perceptual-motor activities than from the traditional free play or competitive-game approach to physical education.

Conclusions and Implications

The hypothesis that perceptual-motor development programs positively influence reading achievement can neither be confirmed nor denied on the basis of the research reviewed here. This, however, is a generalization. What is more important is specification of the objectives and conditions under which any educational activity is undertaken. Thus, it seems that individualized perceptual-motor programs are developmentally appropriate for disadvantaged children as a preventive program or for some children with learning disabilities as a remedial program. When perceptual-motor development programs are used for all children without reference to their prior environmental experiences or needs, any positive influence upon reading is doubtful. The inclusion of perceptual-motor activities in lieu of free play and game-oriented physical education in day care, early childhood education, or primary programs is desirable. The best advice for the teacher responsible for facilitating opportunities for a person to exercise his "right to read" is to consider perceptual-motor programs as being a supplement—*not a substitute*—for competent reading instruction.

References and Notes

1. Braley, William T. "Longitudinal Study of the Effects of Sensorimotor Training in Preschool." Dayton Public Schools, 1970, and personal correspondence, 1971.

2. Cohen, S. Alan. "Studies in Visual Perception and Reading in Disadvantaged Children," *Journal of Learning Disabilities,* 2 (1969), 498-503.

3. Gessell, A. "The Ontogenesis of Infant Behavior," in L. Carmichael (Ed.), *Manual of Child Psychology.* New York: John Wiley and Sons, 1946.

4. Faustman, Marion N. "Some Effects of Perception Training in Kindergarten on First Grade Success in Reading," in Helen K. Smith (Ed.), *Perception and Reading,* 1967 Proceedings, Volume 12, Part 4. Newark, Delaware: International Reading Association, 1968, 99-101.

5. Fisher, David M. "Effects of Two Different Types of Physical Education Programs Upon Skills Developed and Academic Readiness of Kindergarten Children," doctoral dissertation, Louisiana State University, 1970.

6. Klesius, Stephen E. "Perceptual-Motor Development and Reading," *Proceedings of the College Reading Association,* 11, 1970, 37-44.

7. Litchfield, Ticknor B. "A Program of Visual-Motor-Perceptual Training to Determine Its Effects Upon Primary Level Children with

Learning Deficiencies." Suffern, New York: Ramapo Central School District, 1970. (ERIC ED 043-994.)

8. McCulloch, Lovell. "Physical Education Perceptual-Motor Training Program for Kindergarten Children." Wisconsin: Ripon Public Schools, 1969.
9. McGraw, M. "Maturation of Behavior," in L. Carmichael (Ed.), *Manual of Child Psychology*. New York: John Wiley and Sons, 1946.
10. McRaney, Kenneth A. "A Study of Perceptual-Motor Exercises Utilized as an Early Grade Enrichment Program for the Improvement of Learning Activity and Motor Development," doctoral dissertation, University of Southern Mississippi, 1970. *Dissertation Abstracts,* 31 (1970) 3935-A.
11. New Jersey State Department of Education. "A Study in Visual-Motor Perceptual Training in the First Grade," Department of Education, 1965. (ERIC ED 031-292.)
12. O'Connor, Colleen. "The Effects of Physical Activities Upon Motor Ability, Perceptual Ability, and Academic Achievement of First Graders," *Dissertation Abstracts,* 30 (1968), 4310-A.
13. Piaget, Jean. *The Origins of Intelligence in Children.* New York: International University Press, 1952.
14. Siegel, A. "A Motor Hypothesis of Perceptual Development," *American Journal of Psychology,* 66 (1953), 301-304.
15. Slacks, Rosemary. "The Effects of Physical Activities Upon Perceptual Abilities, Reading Ability, and Academic Achievement," master's thesis, University of Texas, 1969.
16. Smith, Karl U., and William M. Smith. *Perception and Motion: An Analysis of Space Structured Behavior.* Philadelphia: W.B. Saunders, 1962.
17. Turner, Robert V., and Maurice D. Fisher. "The Effect of a Perceptual-Motor Training Program Upon the Readiness and Perceptual Development of Culturally Disadvantaged Kindergarten Children." Richmond, Virginia: Public Schools, 1970. (ERIC ED 041-633.)
18. Weisman, Eva A., and Mary R. Leonard. "A Multi-Disciplinary Approach to the Development of Verbal and Reading Skills." Baltimore City Public Schools, 1969, and personal correspondence, 1970.

Betty Piercy
Iowa City, Iowa, Schools

finds some answers to questions concerning perceptual-discrimination skills.

STRATEGIES FOR DEVELOPING READINESS FOR INDEPENDENCE IN WORD RECOGNITION

Each decade brings forth new ideas and new techniques for the teaching of reading, and the decade of the seventies promises to be no exception. Indications are that it may be the most fruitful of any era as time, energy, and money are put into the "Right to Read" program.

The strategies for developing readiness for independence in word recognition have changed somewhat from those of the previous decade. This may be a result of the first grade studies and other research that followed. A variety of approaches are available—developmental, phonic, linguistic, orthographic stress, language experience, individualized reading, and some other specialized approaches—with each consisting of a number of systems or sets of parts coordinated to accomplish a particular set of objectives. The only valid reason for developing such strategies to achieve readiness for and eventually independence in word recognition is to ultimately accomplish the complex task of reading.

Reading is, indeed, a complex task inasmuch as it involves interaction between the reader and the written language to the extent that the reader reacts to the message of the writer. If reading were merely perception of words without conceptual learning, it might be defined as word identification. Such a definition is inadequate, for comprehension must occur even in the beginning stages of decoding the written language.

Materials used to teach reading should be those that offer a child an opportunity to experience the joy and fulfillment of expection in learning to read. If weeks go by in which the child merely works on identifying letters of the alphabet, letter-sound associations, and/or identification of words in a fixed spelling pattern, his interest may soon be lost to such an extent that it is impossible to motivate that child to a successful reading experience.

From infancy until entry into school, be it preschool, kindergarten, or first grade, many factors play an influencing role on developing readiness for independence in word recognition.

Weintraub (*21*) defines the concept for readiness for reading as the interweaving of numerous factors—physical, social, emotional, mental, and language—that help a child succeed in learning to read.

Children's language patterns develop very early through imitation, but other influencing factors require some planning by those responsible for early training. Children having opportunities to explore many areas in the community and to accompany their parents on trips will be equipped with a vast number of already formed concepts that will assist in interpreting the printed page.

Reading Stories to Children

One of the best strategies for developing this desired readiness is reading aloud to children, for it offers them an opportunity to hear good literature, to develop good listening habits, to observe others engaged in the act of reading, and to understand what reading is.

As children listen to the stories read to them, their eyes may follow along the lines. They become aware of individual words, understand that words ordered in a particular sequence have certain meanings, learn to anticipate what comes next, receive an introduction to the left-to-right and top-to-bottom progression needed for reading, and acquire the knowledge that much pleasure can be obtained from printed language.

The read-along technique is employed by some basal programs and in some materials prepared for listening centers using books accompanied by tapes or records.

According to Robinson (*14*) "The primary purpose of reading along is to motivate a desire for learning to read and to expose children to written language." Children gain confidence and experience success with this procedure.

Pictures correlated with the narrative of a story in either basal reading material or trade books provide cues for recognizing words and giving meaning to a word or to a larger part of the context.

Children apparently have three learning or neurological systems which are correlated in the learning process, namely, auditory, visual, and tactual—kinaesthetic.

Auditory-Perceptual Discrimination

The majority of children learn by any modality and have only slight preference, and it seems impractical to attempt to test and classify *all* children. However, if a child exhibits difficulties with learning to read, appraisal of the different modalities involved in the instruction should be made.

Wepman (*22*) found that the audile child has an adequacy of speech articulation, is sensitive to sound, reacts to fine differences in voices, responds to spoken requests, ignores visual stimuli, and appears to daydream when only visual material is presented. The visile child may watch a speaker, yet pay little or no attention to what is being said, but is inquisitive about books and pictures. The tactile child loves to use his hands, performs well with puzzles, seems to be preoccupied with what he is doing, and fails to listen or look at people when he is addressed.

For some children, the auditory modality proves the only available means of teaching the necessary skills and social attitudes while other children, according to Wepman (*23*), may be so deficient in that area that for most situations the children are functionally deaf even though their hearing acuity is quite normal.

The audile child may be ready to read when he first comes to school if instruction is given to him verbally. If he shows a strong preference for the visual modality, he may learn easily by a sight method but have difficulty with a method having a strong letter-sound emphasis. The tactual-kinaesthetic child will tend to make more rapid progress using a writing approach to reading.

Frostig (*3*) states that numerous reading difficulties occur because of the many skills involved in the reading process and that a deficit in any one of them might cause a problem. She lists the following skills as those involved: 1) sensory-motor skills such as eye movement, control for scanning, and finger control for turning pages; 2) auditory-perceptual skills; 3) visual-perceptual skills; 4) language skills; and 5) the ability to think logically, draw conclusions, and make inferences.

Visual-Perceptual Discrimination

Weiner, Wepman, and Morency (*20*) in 1965 and Weinter (*19*) in 1968 report conclusions that discrimination of visual forms is one of skills prerequisite to reading.

Studies by Goin (*4*) and Cohen (*2*) indicate that visual training produced gains in visual-discrimination tasks but held no carryover into reading. Other research shows that prereading activities in visual discrimination is of greater value if practice is provided with letter and word discrimination rather than with pictures, geometrical forms, and designs.

From Barrett's review (*1*) of the research on visual discrimination, one may conclude that the more the visual discrimination task resembles the reading task, the better predictor of reading achievement it will be.

Before a child is able to learn to recognize words, it will be necessary for him to have adequate visual-perceptual ability.

In the beginning stages of reading there is a positive correlation between visual-perceptual abilities and reading, but, according to Weintraub (*21*), that relationship lessens after the child has been in school several years. It is not that the visual-perceptual abilities are no longer important but, that children are able to discriminate likenesses and differences among words well enough that measures of that skill are not useful in distinguishing the more able from the less able readers.

The visual modality, like the auditory, develops in a predictable manner from discrimination to memory and through sequential order. Visual-perceptual abilities are usually developed before children enter school. Many children, however, need instruction in attending to the things being discriminated, and this, then, becomes another important strategy in reaching the goal for independence in reading.

Reading requires more than visual perception; one of the abilities being auditory perception. Morency (*12*) found that there is consistent growth in auditory discrimination and memory until it reaches fruition in about the ninth year and that auditory measures are not, in themselves, predictors of success or failure in reading.

The Linguistic Influence

The linguists have had a great influence on many of the reading programs currently in use and those just being released by their publishers.

Wardhaugh (*17*), Goodman (*5*), and Shuy (*16*) all suggest that there is no linguistic method of reading instruction. Linguistics is the science of language and as such offers insights into the reading process and reading instruction, but it does not offer a method nor even an approach to reading.

Goodman (*6*) is of the opinion that it is necessary to change the point of focus if the new knowledge about language is to be utilized. He believes we can no longer be preoccupied with letters and words. He (*7*) calls reading a psycholinguistic guessing game which ". . . involves an interaction between thought and language." He states:

> Efficient reading does not result from precise perception and identification of all elements, but from skill in selecting the fewest, most productive

> cues necessary to produce guesses which are right the first time. The ability to anticipate that which has not been seen, of course, is vital to reading, just as the ability to anticipate what has not yet been heard is vital to listening.

Even with considerable instruction some first grade children do not understand what a word is. Perhaps teachers should move away from word-centeredness in materials and instructions and move toward more careful development of word sense. Then the goal, according to Goodman (*8*), "becomes effective reading for more complete comprehension. Instead of word attack skills, sight vocabularies, and word perception, the program must be designed to build comprehension strategies." He also states that ". . . first, a learner knows a graphic sentence; then he knows familiar words in new sentences; and, finally, he knows words anywhere, including lists."

Research shows that phonics instruction results in superior reading achievement later. Wardhaugh (*18*) asks if existing phonics methods are better than other methods in teaching beginning reading, then how much better would a phonics method based on linguistically defensible information be.

Children rely heavily on the structure of language in utilizing the predictability factor to unlock new words, and beginning reading materials should include as much linguistic redundancy as possible, according to both Goodman (*9*) and Shuy (*16*).

Goodman (*10*) states "what is most important in beginning reading is not the particular word but the development of strategies to use in subsequent situations."

Other Clues

It is easier to read and learn words in context than in isolation. Actually, there are two contexts, syntactical (grammar) and semantic (meaning) which work together to help a reader get the meaning of a word or words. Thus, three cues are available to the reader in determining new words, and to become competent the reader will need to use all cues—syntactic, semantic, and phonemic-graphemic.

Children discriminate words by letter differences rather than by shape or some other cue. The first letter of the word is the most important cue, and the last letter is the second most important one.

Williams (*24*) found that children receiving concurrent training in multiple phoneme-grapheme correspondence tend to use a problem-solving approach in trying out various pronunciations when meeting an unfamiliar word.

Each skill or step toward mastery of reading should be overlearned until the use of it becomes a habit.

No plan would be complete without strategies for getting the pupils into a program of independent, personal, self-selected reading at the earliest moment. Improvement in the reading skills may be most noticeable when children read widely on subjects of their particular interests.

In addition to the strategies suggested here, teachers must have *time* to teach; children must have *time* to learn; and both teachers and children need *time to read.*

References

1. Barrett, Thomas C. "The Relationship between Measures of Prereading Visual Discrimination and First Grade Reading Achievement: A Review of the Literature," *Reading Research Quarterly,* 1 (Fall 1965), 51-76.
2. Cohen, Ruth I. "Remedial Training of First Grade Children with Visual Perceptual Retardation," *Educational Horizons,* 45 (Winter 1966-1967), 60-63.
3. Frostig, Marianne. "Visual Modality, Research and Practice," in Helen K. Smith (Ed.), *Perception and Reading.* Newark, Delaware: International Reading Association, 1968, 25-33.
4. Goins, Jean Turner. *Visual Perceptual Abilities and Early Reading Progress,* Supplementary Educational Monographs, No. 87. Chicago: University of Chicago, 1958.
5. Goodman, Kenneth S. "Is the Linguistic Approach an Improvement in Reading Instruction?" in Nila Banton Smith (Ed.), *Current Issues in Reading.* Newark, Delaware: International Reading Association, 1969, 268-276.
6. Goodman, Kenneth S. (Ed.). *The Psycholinguistic Nature of the Reading Process.* Detroit: Wayne State University Press, 1968, 15-26.
7. Goodman, Kenneth S. "Reading: A Psycholinguistic Guessing Game," in Harry Singer and Robert B. Ruddell (Eds.), *Theoretical Models and Processes of Reading.* Newark, Delaware: International Reading Association, 1970, 259-272.
8. Goodman, Kenneth S. "Words and Morphemes in Reading," in Ken-

neth S. Goodman and James T. Fleming (Eds.), *Psycholinguistics and the Teaching of Reading.* Newark, Delaware: International Reading Association, 1969, 25-33.

9. Goodman, Kenneth S., et al. *Choosing Materials to Teach Reading.* Detroit: Wayne State University Press, 1966.
10. Goodman, Yetta M. "Using Children's Reading Miscues for New Teaching Strategies," *Reading Teacher,* 23 (February 1970), 455-459.
11. King, Ethel M., and Siegmar Muehl. "Different Sensory Cues as Aid in Beginning Reading," *Reading Teacher,* 19 (December 1965), 163-168.
12. Morency, Anne. "Auditory Modality, Research, and Practice," in Helen K. Smith (Ed.), *Perception and Reading.* Newark, Delaware: International Reading Association, 1968, 17-21.
13. Robinson, Helen M. (Ed.). *Coordinating Reading Instruction.* Glenview, Illinois: Scott, Foresman, 1971.
14. Robinson, Helen M., et al. *Ready to Roll,* Teacher's Manual. Glenview, Illinois: Scott, Foresman, 1967.
15. Samuels, S. Jay. "Attentional Process in Reading: The Effect of Pictures on the Acquisition of Reading Responses," *Journal of Educational Psychology,* 58 (December 1967), 337-342.
16. Shuy, Roger W. "Some Relationships of Linguistics to the Reading Process," *A Duck Is a Duck, Helicopters and Gingerbread* (Teacher's Edition), Theodore Clymer, et al. Boston: Ginn, 1969, 8-15.
17. Wardhaugh, Ronald. "Is the Linguistic Approach an Improvement in Reading Instruction?" in Nila Banton Smith (Ed.), *Current Issues in Reading.* Newark, Delaware: International Reading Association, 1969, 254-267.
18. Wardhaugh, Ronald. "The Teaching of Phonics and Comprehension: A Linguistic Evaluation," in Kenneth S. Goodman and James T. Fleming (Eds.), *Psycholinguistics and the Teaching of Reading.* Newark, Delaware: International Reading Association, 1969, 79-90.
19. Weiner, Paul S. "A Revision of the Chicago Test of Visual Discrimination," *Elementary School Journal,* 68 (April 1968), 370-380.
20. Weiner, Paul S., Joseph Wepman, and Anne S. Morency. "A Test of Visual Discrimination," *Elementary School Journal,* 65 (March 1965), 330-337.
21. Weintraub, Samuel. "What Research Says About Learning to Read," in Helen M. Robinson (Ed.), *Coordinating Reading Instruction.* Glenview, Illinois: Scott, Foresman, 1971, 180-201.
22. Wepman, Joseph M. "Modalities and Learning," in Helen M. Robinson

(Ed.), *Coordinating Reading Instruction.* Glenview, Illinois: Scott, Foresman, 1971, 55-60.

23. Wepman, Joseph M. "The Modality Concept—Including a Statement of the Perceptual and Conceptual Levels of Learning," in Helen K. Smith (Ed.), *Perception and Reading.* Newark, Delaware: International Reading Association, 1968, 1-6.
24. Williams, Joanna P. "Successive Versus Concurrent Presentation of Multiple Grapheme-Phoneme Correspondences," *Journal of Educational Psychology,* 59 (October 1968), 309-314.

IS SILENT READING THE "BEST" STRATEGY WHEN LANGUAGE IS ESSENTIALLY PHONEMIC?

WILLIAM C. DAVIES
Shippensburg State College

provides a negative answer and supports it with research.

IMPLICIT SPEECH—SOME CONCLUSIONS DRAWN FROM RESEARCH

One of the main thrusts of research on learning during the sixties was an intensive reexamination of language development in infancy and early childhood. Piaget, Gagne, Tolman, Bruner, and others suggest answers to today's burning questions: "How soon and through which mode(s) does a child develop language?" Prerequisite to further understanding of this faculty is a better analysis of the phenomenon of implicit speech.

Implicit speech compounds its confused image by covert behavior—silent speech, subvocalism, and inner speech—and overt behavior—lip movements, faint whispering of many words, and saying every word. The basic concept inherent in all of these terms is that implicit speech is inseparable from any act of thinking itself, as well as being concomitant to any instance of speaking, listening, reading, or writing. It may be rewarding, therefore, to overview the century long experimental and clinical studies of implicit speech and to assess the implications of recently completed research in this area.

A Brief Experimental History

Consideration of implicit speech began in 1868 when Bain and Ribat (*2*), physiological psychologists, proposed that thinking is more or less restrained vocalization or acting. Curtis (*7*) in 1899 bandaged a tambour over the larynx to record movements simulated by silent reading. He concluded that silent reading produced considerably more movement than any other mental activity. A telegraph key device activated by the tip of the tongue through a suction cup was devised by Tomor (*25*). He concluded, "All thinking is accompanied by activity in the musculature of these (speech) organs." Work with a small rubber balloon and a pneumograph connected to a kymograph caused Scheck (*21*) to announce that mental stress heightens tongue activity and that this activity varies in rates and amounts.

A significant breakthrough came in 1950 when Edfelt (*11*) used rubber bulbs attached to an Elmquist Mingograph (an electronically activated direct-wiring instrument) to record movements. He concluded, "New techniques (electromyography) are needed for any further progress." A decade later he published *Silent Speech and Silent Reading* (*11*), in which he reports the only comprehensive, adequately instrumented, and scientifically controlled study of the fifties. His conclusions are, "Silent speech is universal during silent reading; it increases with the difficulty of the material; *efforts to eliminate it should be discontinued.*"

Edfelt formed three hypotheses:

1. Good readers engage in less silent speech than do poor ones.
2. The reading of an easy text results in less silent speech than does the reading of a difficult one.
3. The reading of a clear text results in less silent speech than does the reading of a blurred one.

Clinical Application of Experimental Results

Yoakam (*28*) quotes Smith (*23*) as follows: "It must be borne in mind, however, that the written word is a mere transposition of the spoken word and that the two are intimately associated. . . . It is, therefore, not surprising that the perception of the written word should be accompanied by some degree of articulation and hearing." Yoakam summarizes in his book *Reading and Study,* as follows:

1. The process of vocalization goes on even in silent reading in the case of most, if not all, readers.
2. The amount of vocalization varies with the reader.
3. Lip movements accompany the silent reading of young children and also of inefficient adult readers.
4. It is thought by some that vocalization of a perceptible sort is unnecessary and could be avoided by the right kind of training.

Cole (*6*) codes five stages of vocalization in a reader as follows:

1. Saying or whispering every word.
2. Faint whispering of many words.

3. Pronounced lip movement but no sound.
4. No lip movement or sound, but palpable movement of the tongue.
5. No lip movement, sound, or palpable movement of tongue, but palpable movement of the throat.

To the above stages Edfelt would have added a sixth:

6. No movements discernible except by electromyography.

Causation Theories of Implicit Speech

A major area of inquiry has been the causes of implicit speech:

1. In 1900, Secor (*22*) considered "inner speech" of children and poor readers as distinct from "inner hearing."
2. In 1908, Huey (*15*) stated: "For the readers tested . . . it seemed that inner speech was a combination of auditory and motor elements, with one or the other predominating according to the reader's habitual mode of learning."
3. In 1914, Watson (*27*) hypothesized that implicit speech might be physiologically required as a factor in the process of reading.
4. In 1947, Gates (*12*) proposed the theory that implicit speech, being a motor habit, originates in earlier training and experience in oral reading.
5. In 1950, Betts (*3*) suggested that lip movers use silent speech which mechanically restrains the silent reading rate. Bond and Bond (*4*) concur with Betts.
6. More recently, DeBoer and Dallman (*10*) observed that after a pupil has learned to read more rapidly silently than orally, vocalization is a detriment to the rate of silent reading.
7. McKim (*17*) feels that vocalization is properly frowned upon as a hindrance to reading speed, but it is not necessary to become disturbed if a good reader occasionally resorts to this device.

The accumulated opinions of specialists in the field of reading, as these samples indicate, support the theory that implicit speech may aid comprehension in the primary grades but that it can be a deterrent to adequate rate in the intermediate and upper grades.

To eliminate or inhibit implicit speech, O'Brien (*18*), McDade (*16*), and Buswell (*5*), suggest nonoral methods of reading instruction. McDade's program was administered in the Chicago Public Schools. The results are inconclusive and disappointing; the nonoral method did not eliminate implicit speech to any greater degree than did any other method.

It has been suggested that implicit speech is a developmental reinforcement activity and would be eliminated or reduced to a minimum, according to Hollingsworth's cue-reduction theory (*14*), by increasing the rate of silent reading.

Finally, as the cumulative fruition of those decades of investigation and experiment, Anderson and Dearborn (*1*), seconded by Tinker (*24*), in 1952 made the revolutionary recommendation that implicit speech is a desirable, developmental, learning reinforcement activity and that its elimination should not be prematurely precipitated. This position was acclaimed by Edfelt (*11*) in 1960.

Implicit Speech Research 1960-1970

An exhaustive search of the literature in addition to query of the Eric/Crier data base reveals nine major investigations central to implicit speech from 1960 to 1970. Three which have direct bearing on implicit speech as a covert-overt form of linguistic behavior in beginning reading are set forth in the Eric/Crier Document Resumé format as follows:

1. ED 027 154-24-RE 001 519. Cleland, Donald L., and others. *Vocalism in Silent Reading,* Final Report. University of Pittsburgh, School of Education, 1968.
2. ED 012 682 RE 000 195. Laffey, James L. *Behavioral Research That Has Promise in the Teaching of Reading.* University of Pittsburgh, School of Education, 1966.
3. ED 022 656-24-RE 001 441. Hardyck, Curtis D. *The Effect of Subvocal Speech on Reading,* Final Report. Berkeley: University of California, 1968.

The results of these studies can be summarized.

Cleland (*8*) satisfies Edfelt's criterion demand (*11*) that better instrumentation in electromyography (including quantification validation by electronic integrator-circuit recorders) is necessary for further research productivity. He also qualitatively endorses the contentions of Anderson and Dearborn (*1*), Tinker (*24*), and Edfelt (*11*), that implicit speech is a normal adjunct to the reading process; that it is a natural developmental comprehension reinforcer; and that, consequently, classroom techniques for its repression should be minimized, if not abandoned altogether.

Laffey performed a descriptive study of the previous parameters of implicit speech research superimposed upon the new framework of interdisciplinary behavioral study that came into vogue in the first half of the 1960-1970 decade. He attempts to relate how this new interdisciplinary behavioral research

1. applies basic scientific techniques to practical learning situations;
2. helps bridge the gap between learning theory and practical classroom application;
3. represents an interdisciplinary attack on educational problems; and
4. encompasses the essential task of education—behavioral change.

Laffey's contribution in synthesizing the previously known but jumbled mass of experimental data into a codified and meaningful context is a significant one. He provides points of entry from each of the five behavioral sciences involved. Of particular value are his bridges from scientific techniques to learning theory to practical classroom application.

Hardyck essentially replicates Edfelt's college-level comprehension-testing design done at the University of Stockholm in 1960 (*11*). His experimental study was well-designed and competently executed. His findings do, in fact, support many of the hypotheses which Edfelt recommends for further testing. However, because the levels of development concerned are college and secondary, Hardyck's research does not have the degree of applicability to the process of learning to read as do Cleland's (*8*) and Laffey's.

Conclusions

The century of interest in implicit speech as a correlate of language acquisition in general and beginning reading in particular, from Bain and Ribat (*2*) in 1868 to Laffey in 1968, has proved to be an intriguing and fruitful epoch. Based upon the preceding evaluation of the pertinent evidence available, a concluding statement is directed to each of three classes of educational practitioners:

1. Learning Theorists. Current reassessments of learning theory of Piaget (*20*) and Bruner (*19*) suggest that in infancy and early childhood a precocity and sophistication of learning through ap-

plication of language skills exist to a greater extent than has been previously suspected.

2. Psycholinguists. Every shred of evidence in the past decade from Goodman (*13*) to Wardhaugh (*26*) highlights a glittering metallic thread of inner language activity weaving through the entire fabric of human thinking responsive to external (and internal) stimuli from the "first birth cry of language expression" onward.
3. Classroom teachers. A final reiteration of the yield of this century of scholarly inquiry into the nature of implicit speech which has potential for benefit to the art of the teaching of beginning reading is appropriate. Anderson and Dearborn (*1*), Tinker (*24*), Edfelt (*11*), and Cleland and Davies (*8*) reinforce to the point of conviction that, "Implicit speech is a desirable, developmental learning reinforcement activity; its elimination should *not* be prematurely precipitated."

References

1. Anderson, Irving H., and Walter F. Dearborn. *The Psychology of Teaching Reading.* New York: Ronald Press, 1952, 160.

2. Bain, Alexander. *The Senses and the Intellect* (3rd ed.). London: Longmans, Green, 1868.

3. Betts, Emmett A. *Foundations of Reading Instruction.* New York: American Book, 1950.

4. Bond, Guy L., and Eva Bond. *Developmental Reading in High School.* New York: Macmillan, 1950, 326.

5. Buswell, Guy T. "The Subvocalization Factor in the Improvement of Reading," *Elementary School Journal,* 48 (1947), 190-196.

6. Cole, Luella. *The Improvement of Reading.* New York: Farrar and Rinehart, 1938, 29.

7. Curtis, H. S. "Automatic Movements of the Larynx," *American Journal of Psychology,* 11 (1900), 237-239.

8. Cleland, Donald L., and William C. Davies. "Silent Speech—History and Current Status," *Reading Teacher,* January 1963.

9. Davies, William C. "Silent Speech: Its Development and Current Status in Experimental Research, Clinical Practice, and Classroom Application," unpublished doctoral dissertation, School of Education, University of Pittsburgh, 1962.

10. De Boer, John J., and Martha Dallman. *The Teaching of Reading.* New York: Holt, Rinehart and Winston, 1960, 155.
11. Edfelt, Ake W. *Silent Speech and Silent Reading.* Chicago: University of Chicago Press, 1960.
12. Gates, Arthur I. *The Improvement of Reading.* New York: Macmillan, 1947.
13. Goodman, Kenneth S., and James T. Fleming. *Psycholinguistics and the Teaching of Reading.* Newark, Delaware: International Reading Association, 1969.
14. Hollingsworth, H. L. *Educational Psychology.* New York: Appleton-Century, 1933, 540.
15. Huey, E. B. *The Psychology and Pedagogy of Reading.* New York: Macmillan, 1908.
16. McDade, James E. "A Hypothesis for Non-Oral Reading: Argument, Experiment, and Results," *Journal of Educational Research,* 30 (March 1937), 489-503.
17. McKim, Margaret G. *Guiding Growth in Reading.* New York: Macmillan, 1955, 411.
18. O'Brien, John A. *Silent Reading.* New York: Macmillan, 1921.
19. Pines, Maya. "Jerome Bruner Maintains—Infants Are Smarter Than Anybody Thinks," *New York Times,* November 1970.
20. Raven, Ronald J., and Richard T. Salzer. "Piaget and Reading Instruction," *Reading Teacher* (April 1971), 630.
21. Scheck, M. "Involuntary Tongue Movements Under Varying Stimuli," *Proceedings of the Iowa Academy of Sciences,* 32 (1925), 385-391.
22. Secor, W. "Visual Reading: A Study in Mental Imagery," *American Journal of Psychology,* 11 (1900), 225-236.
23. Smith, W. A. *The Reading Process.* New York: Macmillan, 1922.
24. Tinker, Miles A. *Teaching Elementary Reading.* New York: Appleton-Century, 1952, 14.
25. Tomor, E. "Die Rolle der Muskein beim Denken," *Archiv für die gesamte Psychologie,* 12 (1910), 362-366.
26. Wardhaugh, Ronald. *Reading: A Linguistic Perspective.* Harcourt, Brace and World, 1969.
27. Watson, J. B. *Behavior: An Introduction to Comparative Psychology.* New York: Holt, 1914.
28. Yoakam, Gerald A. *Reading and Study.* New York: Macmillan, 1928.